The Writings of Frithjof Schuon
Series

World Wisdom
The Library of Perennial Philosophy

The Library of Perennial Philosophy is dedicated to the exposition of the timeless Truth underlying the diverse religions. This Truth, often referred to as the *Sophia Perennis*—or Perennial Wisdom—finds its expression in the revealed Scriptures as well as the writings of the great sages and the artistic creations of the traditional worlds.

Gnosis: Divine Wisdom, A New Translation with Selected Letters appears as one of our selections in the Writings of Frithjof Schuon series.

The Writings of Frithjof Schuon

The Writings of Frithjof Schuon form the foundation of our library because he is the preeminent exponent of the Perennial Philosophy. His work illuminates this perspective in both an essential and comprehensive manner like none other.

English Language Writings of Frithjof Schuon

Original Books
The Transcendent Unity of Religions
Spiritual Perspectives and Human Facts
Gnosis: Divine Wisdom
Language of the Self
Stations of Wisdom
Understanding Islam
Light on the Ancient Worlds
Treasures of Buddhism (In the Tracks of Buddhism)
Logic and Transcendence
Esoterism as Principle and as Way
Castes and Races
Sufism: Veil and Quintessence
From the Divine to the Human
Christianity/Islam: Essays on Esoteric Ecumenicism
Survey of Metaphysics and Esoterism
In the Face of the Absolute
The Feathered Sun: Plains Indians in Art and Philosophy
To Have a Center
Roots of the Human Condition
Images of Primordial and Mystic Beauty: Paintings by Frithjof Schuon
Echoes of Perennial Wisdom
The Play of Masks
Road to the Heart: Poems
The Transfiguration of Man
The Eye of the Heart
Form and Substance in the Religions
Adastra & Stella Maris: Poems by Frithjof Schuon (bilingual edition)
Autumn Leaves & The Ring: Poems by Frithjof Schuon (bilingual edition)
Songs without Names, Volumes I-VI: Poems by Frithjof Schuon
Songs without Names, Volumes VII-XII: Poems by Frithjof Schuon
World Wheel, Volumes I-III: Poems by Frithjof Schuon
World Wheel, Volumes IV-VII: Poems by Frithjof Schuon
Primordial Meditation: Contemplating the Real

Edited Writings
The Essential Frithjof Schuon, ed. Seyyed Hossein Nasr
Songs for a Spiritual Traveler: Selected Poems (bilingual edition)
René Guénon: Some Observations, ed. William Stoddart
The Fullness of God: Frithjof Schuon on Christianity, ed. James S. Cutsinger
Prayer Fashions Man: Frithjof Schuon on the Spiritual Life, ed. James S. Cutsinger
Art from the Sacred to the Profane: East and West, ed. Catherine Schuon
Splendor of the True: A Frithjof Schuon Reader, ed. James S. Cutsinger

Gnosis: Divine Wisdom

A New Translation with Selected Letters

by

Frithjof Schuon

Includes Other Previously Unpublished Writings

Edited by
James S. Cutsinger

World Wisdom

Gnosis: Divine Wisdom
A New Translation with Selected Letters
© 2006 World Wisdom, Inc.

Translated from the French by Mark Perry, Jean-Pierre Lafouge,
and James S. Cutsinger.

Most recent printing indicated by last digit below
10 9 8 7 6 5 4 3 2

Published in French as
Sentiers de Gnose
La Place Royale, Gaillac, 1996.

Library of Congress Cataloging-in-Publication Data

Schuon, Frithjof, 1907-1998.
  [Sentiers de gnose. English.]
  Gnosis : divine wisdom : a new translation with selected letters / by Frithjof
Schuon ; includes other previously unpublished writings edited by James S.
Cutsinger.
    p. cm. – (The writings of Frithjof Schuon)
  Includes bibliographical references and index.
  ISBN-13: 978-1-933316-18-5 (pbk. : alk. paper)
  ISBN-10: 1-933316-18-7 (pbk. : alk. paper) 1. Religion–Philosophy. I.
Cutsinger, James S., 1953- II. Title. III. Series: Schuon, Frithjof, 1907-1998.
Works. English. 2002.
  BL51.S46573 2006
  200–dc22

                                                              2006014872

Cover Art:
Manjushri, the *Bodhisattva* of Wisdom, from
Frithjof Schuon's private collection.

Printed on acid-free paper in The United States of America.

For information address World Wisdom, Inc.
P.O. Box 2682, Bloomington, Indiana 47402-2682
www.worldwisdom.com

CONTENTS

EDITOR'S PREFACE

We are pleased to present this new edition of Frithjof Schuon's *Gnosis: Divine Wisdom*.

Widely regarded as one of the greatest spiritual writers of the twentieth century, Frithjof Schuon (1907-1998) was an authority on an extraordinary range of religious and philosophical topics, and his books have been praised by scholars and spiritual teachers from many different traditions. He was also the leading representative of the perennialist school of comparative religious thought. Deeply rooted in the *sophia perennis*, *philosophia perennis*, or *religio perennis*—that is, the perennial wisdom, perennial philosophy, or perennial religion, as he variously called it—Schuon's perspective embodies the timeless and universal principles underlying the doctrines, symbols, sacred art, and spiritual practices of the world's religions.

Gnosis: Divine Wisdom was Schuon's fourth major work. Published in Paris in 1957 by La Colombe under the title *Sentiers de Gnose* and first translated in 1959 by G. E. H. Palmer for Perennial Books, the book appeared in a new French edition in 1987, and a third edition, revised and corrected by the author, was published by La Place Royale in 1996. It is upon this most recent version of the text that the present, fully revised translation is based.

Among the special features of this new edition is an appendix containing previously unpublished selections from the author's letters and other private writings. Throughout his life Schuon carried on an extensive correspondence, much of it in response to questions posed by the many inquirers and visitors, from a variety of religious backgrounds, who looked to him for advice; over a thousand of his letters have been preserved. He also composed nearly twelve hundred short spiritual texts for close friends and associates, compiled in his later years as "The Book of Keys". These and other private writings often contained the seeds of ideas that were later developed into published articles and chapters, and it is hoped that the selections included here will afford the reader a glimpse into a new and very rich dimension of this perennial philosopher's message.

The breadth of Schuon's erudition can be somewhat daunting, especially for those not accustomed to reading philosophical and religious works. The pages of his books contain numerous allusions to traditional theological doctrines, important philosophers or spiritual authorities, and the sacred Scriptures of the world's religions, but a citation or other reference is not often provided. A series of editor's notes, organized by chapter and tagged to the relevant page numbers, has therefore been added to this new edition. Dates are provided for historical figures together with brief explanations regarding the significance of their teachings for Schuon, and citations are given for his frequent quotations from the Bible, Koran, and other sacred texts. The Authorized Version of the Bible has been used throughout; since the author made his own translations from the Koran, we have chosen to render his French for these passages directly into English, though the Pickthall interpretation of the Arabic has been given a certain preference when Koranic quotations appear in our editorial notes.

It is customary for the author to employ a number of technical terms in his writings, drawn from a multitude of traditions and involving several languages, including Arabic, Latin, Greek, and Sanskrit. A glossary has therefore been provided as well; here one will find foreign terms and phrases appearing both in Schuon's text and in our editorial notes, together with translations and definitions.

James S. Cutsinger

I

CONTROVERSIES

The Sense of the Absolute in Religions

Religions are separated from each other by barriers of mutual incomprehension, and one of the principal reasons for this seems to be that the sense of the absolute is situated in each case on a different plane, so that points of comparison often prove illusory. Elements resembling one another in form appear in such diverse contexts that their function changes from one case to another, and as a result their nature changes as well, at least to some extent; this is because the infinitude of the possible excludes precise repetition. The sufficient reason for a "new" phenomenon from the point of view of the manifestation of possibilities is, in short, its difference in relation to "antecedent" phenomena; in other words worlds are not made for one another, and the cause of their particularities is also the cause of their diversity, hence of their reciprocal exclusion. We might simply take note of this situation and leave each world to speak in its own language without trying to show that this language is precisely one among others; but we live in an age when the interpenetration of civilizations gives rise to many problems—not new, it is true, but singularly "timely" and "urgent"— and when the diversity of traditional perspectives gives a pretext to those who wish to destroy the very idea of the absolute and the values connected to it. Confronted with a relativism that is growing ever more intrusive, it is necessary to restore to the intelligence a sense of the absolute, even to the point of having to underline for this purpose the relativity in which immutable things are clothed.

*

* *

It seems quite natural to man to generalize the "structure" of his religious conviction: thus the conviction of the Christian results from the divinity of Christ and in turn from the signs that manifest this divinity, then from its power of salvation, and finally from the historical character of all these factors; basing himself exclusively on these criteria and not finding their exact equivalent elsewhere, the Christian will see nothing but improbability outside his own spiritual cosmos. The Muslim will have the same feeling, but in favor of Islam and for a more or less opposite reason: whereas in Christianity the center of religion is the "Word made flesh", of which the Church is only the "mystical body", in the Muslim climate it is Islam as such—the divine Law enveloping man and the whole of society—which is of prime importance; here it is a question of "totality" and not of "center", and the Prophet is not the determining center from which everything flows, but the personification of this totality. It is on the totality that the stress is placed and not on the spokesman, and it is the divine quality of this totality— of this terrestrial crystallization of the celestial Will[1]—together with the inner experience resulting from the practice of his religion, which confers on the Muslim his profound conviction; and let us add that the Koran, while being the "center" or the "Christic" element of the religion, becomes an irresistible element only through its deployment— *al-islâm*—which appears like a system of channels divinely prepared to receive and direct the flow of the human will. While blessedness for the Christian is to cling to the saving divinity of Christ, even to share in his cross, blessedness for the Muslim consists on the contrary in opening out into a totality, in "surrendering" (*aslama*, whence the word *islâm*) his will to God, in "abandoning" it in the mold of a divine Will that encompasses the whole human personality, from the body to the spirit and from birth to the encounter with God.

If Christianity "places God in man" through the mystery of the Incarnation, Judaism in turn "places man in God" through the mystery of the "chosen People"; it is impossible to dissociate the God of the Jews from His people: to speak of Jehovah is to speak of Israel, and conversely. The great Revelation of Monotheism—or the great personal manifestation of God—took place in Israel, and it is this "fact", the mystery of Sinai, together with the choosing of this people, which gives to the believing Jew his unshakable conviction and constitutes for him that "element of the absolute" without which no religious faith is possible.

For the Christian the overwhelming argument is the divinity of Christ and, flowing from this, the fact that there is an intermediary between God and man in the form of God made man, not to men-

---

[1] This Will is here conceived as "divine Word" and "uncreated Book" at one and the same time.

tion another intermediary, the Mother of God; but if the argument of divinity presupposes that the value of the message should be made to depend on this divinity, the argument of proximity presupposes that God is remote, which is clearly true, though not in every respect. Islam starts precisely from the idea that the infinitely transcendent God is at the same time infinitely close—"closer than your jugular vein"—so that in religious experience He surrounds us and penetrates us, like a sort of luminous ether, if one may use such an imaginative expression; the only necessary intermediary is our own attitude, *al-islâm*, the central element of which is prayer in all its forms. The Judaic God was "remote", but He dwelt among His people and sometimes spoke to them; the Christian God—as God-Man—is the "intermediary" between this remote God and man, this God who is thenceforth silent and merciful; and as for the God of Islam, He is "near" (*al-Qarîb*) without being "human". These are not different Gods, of course; it is solely a question of different perspectives and of the "divine attitudes" corresponding to them. God is always and everywhere God, and this is why each of these attitudes is to be found in its own way in the heart of the other two; there is always, in one mode or another, both "remoteness" and "proximity", just as there is always an "intermediary element".

The sense of the absolute is not grafted onto exactly the same organic element in one religion as it is in another—whence the impossibility of making comparisons between the elements of religions simply from the outside—and this fact is shown clearly by the differing natures of conversions to Christianity and Islam: whereas conversion to Christianity seems in certain respects like the beginning of a great love, which makes all of a man's past life look vain and trivial—it is a "rebirth" after a "death"—conversion to Islam on the contrary is like awakening from an unhappy love, or like sobriety after drunkenness, or again like the freshness of morning after a night of distress. In Christianity the soul is "freezing to death" in its congenital egoism, and Christ is the central fire that warms and restores it to life; in Islam on the other hand the soul is "suffocating" in the constriction of the same egoism, and Islam appears as the cool immensity of space that allows it to "breathe" and "expand" toward the boundless. The "central fire" is denoted by the cross, the "immensity of space" by the Kaaba, the prayer-rug, the abstract interlacings of Islamic art.

In a word, the faith of the Christian is a "concentration" and that of the Muslim an "expansion" (*bast, inshirâh*), as the Koran moreover states;[2] but each of these "modes" is necessarily found somewhere within the framework of the "opposing" perspective. "Concentration" or "warmth" reappears in Sufic "love" (*mahabbah*), while "expansion" or "coolness" penetrates into Christian *gnosis* and, in a more general way, into the "peace of Christ" insofar as this peace is the basis of "purity of heart" and contemplation.

To pass from one Asian tradition—Hinduism, Buddhism, or Taoism—to another is in effect no great matter, seeing that the metaphysical content is everywhere quite apparent and even emphasizes the relative nature of the diversities in the various "mythologies"; these traditions—precisely because of their spiritual transparency—readily absorb elements of foreign traditions; the Shinto divinity becomes a *bodhisattva* without change of essence since the names cover universal realities. But inside the framework of the three Semitic traditions, a change of religion almost amounts to a change of planet, for within this framework the divergent "alchemical positions" must rest upon one and the same prophetic and messianic Monotheism, so that the particular form monopolizes the whole man; spiritual "keys" present themselves as exclusive "facts", for they otherwise risk becoming inoperative; *gnosis* alone has the right to be aware that a key is a key.[3]

---

[2] "Have We (God) not expanded [or "opened"] thy breast (O Muhammad) and removed the burden which weighed on thy back?" (*Sûrah* "Solace" [94]:1-3). Again: "He whom God desires to guide, He expands his breast for Islam, and he whom He desires to stray, He constricts his breast and shrinks it" (*Sûrah* "Cattle" [6]:126).

[3] When one looks closely at the intentions hidden behind the verbal formulations, one perceives that the apparent rejection of the divinity of Christ by Islam signifies, not that the perspective of unity denies such a fundamental reality, but that its intellectual structure excludes the Christian formulation; in other words Islam splits in two the person of the God-Man according to the levels to which the two natures belong, and it does so because it considers Being only in its extra-cosmic divinity. This perspective, which cannot fail to take a dogmatic turn, at the same time aims to avoid the danger of a *de facto* "divinizing" of the human individual, that is, the danger of individualist "humanism" with all its consequences; there is a rebound as it were from "deification". From the Muslim point of view, the saying of Christ, "Before Abraham was, I am", signifies that the *Logos*, the uncreated "Word" of God, and consequently the Intellect as such, "precedes" principially

Metaphysical evidence takes precedence over "physical" or "phenomenal" certitude in cases where such a question can arise; on the other hand certitude on this latter level could never weaken or abolish the self-evidence of principles, the eternal "thoughts" of God.

*
*   *

The differences between religions are reflected very clearly in the different forms of sacred art: compared with Gothic art, above all in its "flamboyant" style, Islamic art is contemplative rather than volitive: it is "intellectual" and not "dramatic", and it opposes the cold beauty of geometrical design to the mystical heroism of cathedrals. Islam is the perspective of "omnipresence" ("God is everywhere"), which coincides with that of "simultaneity" ("Truth has always been"); it aims at avoiding any "particularization" or "condensation", any "unique fact" in time and space, although as a religion it necessarily includes an aspect of "unique fact", without which it would be ineffective or even absurd. In other words Islam aims at what is "everywhere center", and this is why, symbolically speaking, it replaces the cross with the cube or the woven fabric: it "decentralizes" and "universalizes" to the greatest possible extent, in the realm of art as in that of doctrine; it is opposed to any individualist mode and hence to any "personalist" mysticism.

To express ourselves in geometrical terms, we could say that a point which seeks to be unique, and which thus becomes an absolute center, appears to Islam—in art as in theology—as a usurpation of the divine absoluteness and therefore as an "association" (*shirk*); there is

---

all temporal, even prophetic and primordial, manifestation. As for the apparent denial of the crucifixion by the Koran, we have always held that this is a question of theology rather than history, and we have encountered the same point of view in a work of Massignon ("Le Christ dans les Evangiles selon al-Ghazzali"): "Abu Hatim, basing himself on the opinion of one of his masters (who is not named), declares that the beginning of the Koranic verse (4:157) in no way denies the crucifixion and that it must be interpreted after taking account of its ending, 'and they did not kill him truly (*yaqînâ*). God raised him to Himself', and, since Jesus died a martyr, remembering the verses (2:154; *cf.* 3:169) on the death of martyrs: 'Do not say of those who have been killed on the way of God that they are dead: but that they are living; although you are not aware of it.'"

only one single center, God, whence the prohibition against "central-izing" images, especially statues; even the Prophet, the human center of the tradition, has no right to a "Christic uniqueness" and is "decen-tralized" by the series of other Prophets; the same is true of Islam—or the Koran—which is similarly integrated in a universal "fabric" and a cosmic "rhythm", having been preceded by other religions—or other "Books"—which it merely restores. The Kaaba, center of the Muslim world, becomes space as soon as one is inside the building: the ritual direction of prayer is then projected toward the four cardinal points. If Christianity is like a central fire, Islam on the contrary resembles a blanket of snow, at once unifying and leveling and having its center everywhere.

*
* *

There is in every religion not only a choice for the will between the hereafter and the here-below, but also a choice for the intelligence between truth and error; there are, however, differences of correlation. Christ is true because he is Savior—whence the importance that the phenomenal element assumes in this case—whereas Islam aims to save by starting from a discernment that is metaphysical in the final analysis (*lâ ilâha illâ 'Llâh*), which is the saving Truth; but whether it is a question of Christianity or Islam or any other traditional form, it is indeed the metaphysical truth which, thanks to its universality, deter-mines the values of things. And because this truth envelops and pen-etrates everything, there is in it neither "here-below" nor "hereafter", nor any choice of the will; only universal essences count, and these are "everywhere and nowhere"; on this plane there is no choice for the will to make, for as Aristotle says, "the soul is all that it knows". This contemplative serenity appears in the abstract freshness of mosques as also in many Romanesque churches and in certain elements of the best Gothic churches, particularly in the rose windows, which are like "mirrors of *gnosis*" in these sanctuaries of love.

At the risk of repeating ourselves, let us return to certain paral-lels: if Christianity can be at least partially defined with the help of the words "miracle", "love", "suffering", Islam will correspond in turn to the triad "truth", "strength", "poverty"; Islamic piety makes one think less of a "center" filled with a sweet and vivifying warmth—this is the Christian *barakah*—than of a "gift" presented in a light that is white and fresh; its spiritual means are dynamic rather than affective, although the differences in this realm are doubtless far from absolute. Muslim asceticism has about it something dry and of the desert, possessing scarcely any of the dramatic attraction of the asceticism of the West; but in its climate of patriarchal poverty there is a musical and lyrical element, which recreates on a different basis the Christian climate.

We said above that Islam aims to base itself on the element "Truth"—that is, it puts the accent there according to its own point of view and intention—and that it is the "impersonal" character of this element which "decentralizes" Islamic "mythology". In Christianity it will doubtless be thought that the "divine Reality"—manifested by Christ—has precedence over "truth", the first being "concrete" and the second "abstract", and this is the case when "truth" is reduced to the level of thought; but we must not lose sight of the fact that we have *a priori* no knowledge of the divine Reality in the absence of metaphysical truth, whatever the degree of our understanding; from another angle, the word "truth" is often taken as synonymous with "reality"—"I am the way, the truth, and the life"—and this is how Islam understands it. It is precisely because we have to begin with no knowledge beyond the "truth" that we have a right to call "true" what is "real", a terminology that in no way prejudices the effective—and eventually "concrete"—quality of our apparently "abstract" knowledge. Be that as it may, the "subjective" manifestation of the Absolute is no less real than its "objective" manifestation: certitude is nothing less than a miracle.

*
* *

A question that inevitably arises here concerns the historicity of the great religious phenomena: should more confidence be placed in a tradition that presents a maximum of historical evidence? To this the reply must be that there is no metaphysical or spiritual difference between a truth manifested by temporal facts and a truth expressed by other symbols, under a mythological form for example; the modes of manifestation correspond to the mental requirements of different human groups. If certain mentalities prefer marvels that are empirically "improbable" over historical "reality", this is precisely because the marvelous—with which moreover no religion can dispense—indicates transcendence in relation to terrestrial facts; we are tempted to say that the aspect of improbability is the sufficient reason for the marvelous, and it is this unconscious need for feeling the essence of things that explains the tendency to exaggerate found among certain peoples: it is like a trace of nostalgia for the Infinite. Miracles are an interference of the marvelous in the sensory realm; whoever admits miracles must also admit the principle of the marvelous as such and even tolerate pious exaggeration on a certain plane. The appropriateness of "mythological" marvels on the one hand and the existence of contradictions between the religions on the other—which do not imply an intrinsic absurdity within a given religion any more than do the internal contradictions found in all religion—show in their own way that, with God, truth lies above all in the symbol's effective power of enlightenment and not in its literalness; and this is all the more evident in that God, whose wisdom goes beyond words, puts multiple meanings into a single expression.[4] An obscurity in expression—whether elliptical or antinomic—often indicates a richness or depth in meaning, and this explains the apparent inconsistencies found in the sacred Scriptures: in this way God manifests His transcendence in relation to the limitations of human logic; human language can be divine only in an indirect way, neither our words nor our logic being on the level of the divine intention. The uncreated Word shatters created speech while at the same time directing it toward concrete and saving truth.

Must one then conclude—on the pretext that principles are more important than phenomena—that a historical basis has in itself less value from a spiritual perspective than a mythological or purely metaphysical basis? Assuredly not, insofar as it is a question of symbolism; what is less valid is attributing a significance to this historical basis it should not have, substituting it for the symbolic truth and metaphysical reality it expresses; nonetheless the importance of historical fact remains intact with regard to sacred institutions. From another point of view, it should be noted that a traditional narrative is always true: the more or less mythical features that are imposed on the historical

---

[4] Just as the blow of a hammer produces a multitude of sparks, so, say the Cabalists, a single word of the *Torah* contains multiple meanings.

life of the Buddha, for instance, are so many ways of expressing spiritual realities that it would be difficult to convey otherwise.[5] In cases where Revelation is most explicitly founded on history, and to the extent this is so, the historical mode is no doubt necessary: in a world that was heir to Jewish "historicism" and Aristotelian empiricism, it was inevitable that Revelation would take the form of an earthly event without the addition of any non-historical symbolism; but we must observe that too great an insistence on historicity—not historicity as such—may somewhat obscure the metaphysical content of sacred facts or their spiritual "transparency" and can even end, in the form of an abusive criticism, by "eroding" history itself and belittling something whose greatness is not understood.[6]

Those who favor rigorous historicity against the mythologies of Asia will doubtless object that historical truth furnishes proofs of the validity of the means of grace: in this context it is necessary to point out, first, that historical proofs precisely could not be completely rigorous in this domain and, second, that tradition as such, with all it includes in the way of symbolism, doctrine, and sanctity—not to mention other more or less indeterminate criteria—furnishes much more unexceptionable proofs of the divine origin and validity of rites; in a sense a tradition's acceptance of a means of grace—and the turning to account of these means in sanctity—is a criterion far more convincing

---

[5] The fact that the life of the Buddha—which is historical in its main features, including certain miracles—retraces the myth of Indra in no way means that it is itself a myth, any more than the prophecies concerning Christ invalidate his historical reality. On the contrary, if the Buddha's first steps after Enlightenment were marked by lotuses, this fact belongs to the subtle order; it is not in any way "unreal".

[6] The more or less "democratic" depreciation of the Holy Virgin, sanctioned by Péguy and many others, is one example of this kind of thing. Another example is the "criticism"—not just "archeological" but even "psychological"—of sacred facts, a fault which is poles apart from intellectuality and which excludes an understanding of the facts in question. Modern exegesis is only a caricature of ancient hermeneutics, if indeed there remains any relationship between them; it consists above all in giving doubts and prejudices the status of dogmas: according to these prejudices, it is "impossible" that a book should be prior to a certain date or that a scribe should have copied a book, even a sacred one, without altering it; quite improper conclusions are drawn from the smallest facts, and the most disproportionate deductions and inductions are allowed even though all the positive data are contrary to these false principles.

than historicity, not to mention the intrinsic value of the Scriptures. History is often incapable of verification; it is tradition, not criticism, that guarantees it, but it guarantees at the same time the validity of non-historical symbolisms. It is the present and permanent miracle of tradition which nullifies the objection that no man living has been a witness of sacred history; saints are its witnesses far more than historians; to deny tradition as the guarantor of truth amounts in the end to asserting that there are effects without causes.

There is doubtless no truth more "exact" than that of history, but what must be stressed is that there is a truth more "real" than that of facts; the higher reality embraces the "exactness", but the latter on the contrary is far from presupposing the former. Historical reality is less "real" than the profound truth it expresses, and which myths likewise express; a mythological symbolism is infinitely more "true" than a fact deprived of symbolism. And this brings us back to what we were saying above, namely, that the mythological or historical appropriateness of the marvelous, like the existence of dogmatic antinomies, serves to show that for God truth is above all in the efficacy of the symbol and not in the "bare fact".

With regard to historicity or its absence, three degrees must be distinguished: mythology, qualified historicity, and exact historicity. We find the first degree in all mythology properly so called, as also in the monotheistic accounts of creation, and the second degree in other "prehistoric" narratives, whether they concern Noah or Jonah or the human *avatâras* of Vishnu.[7] In Judaism rigorous historicity starts perhaps at Sinai; in Christianity it appears in the whole of the New Testament,[8] but not in the apocryphal writings or *Golden Legend*, which

---

[7] The non-human *avatâras* belong in our opinion to mythological symbolism; at the same time it is necessary to avoid putting into this category every phenomenon that is contrary to the experience of our millenium. On this score we would like to remark that we see no logical reason for denying historicity to the loves of the *gopis*, for if such a symbolism is possible it has a right to exist on the plane of facts; there is something analogous in the case of the Song of Solomon, where the literal meaning, since it exists, keeps all its rights; moral interest must not be confused with the truth, which runs through all the levels of Existence.

[8] One may note, however, the existence of a certain fluctuation, for example on the subject of the "three Mary Magdalenes", as also some contradictory features in the Gospel stories, which seem to us to indicate that sacred things, though being

moreover are not canonical works, a fact which has earned them a disregard that is quite undeserved, symbolism being an essential vehicle of truth; finally, in Islam exact historicity belongs to the life of the Prophet and his Companions, as well as to those of their sayings (*ahâdîth*) recognized by the tradition,[9] but not to stories concerning pre-Islamic Prophets and events, which are woven of symbols that are certainly "exact" but more or less "mythical"; to take them literally, however, is always to be inspired by their "alchemical" virtue even when a real understanding is lacking.[10]

situated here in time, are beyond history; such "irregularities" are in no way contrary to the divine Will, and they are found in any case in sacred art as well where they are like "openings", safeguarding the indefinite flux of "life"; this amounts to saying that every form is inadequate in the eyes of Heaven. There is something of this also in the extreme freedom of scriptural quotations in the New Testament: the divine Speech, in crystallizing itself, is at the same time reluctant to commit itself to certain "fixations". Simply reading the Gospels is enough, from our point of view, to reduce to nothing all the artificial arguments aimed at ruining the authenticity of the texts. Those who, contrary to tradition, extol the value of "criticism" or "objective analysis" forget the essential, namely intelligence, without which the best of methods is futile—even though intelligence is often identified with a critical attitude, as if to doubt a piece of evidence were a sufficient proof of being intelligent.

[9] According to a very widespread opinion, almost all the sayings and deeds of the Prophet recorded by the *sunnah* are falsifications produced by certain interested theologians. The psychological improbability of such a hypothesis is ignored, and it seems to be forgotten that the supposed falsifiers were men who believed in Islam and feared hell; no weight is given to tradition or orthodox unanimity, of course, and this proves an ignorance of what is possible in a tradition and what is not; basically it shows ignorance of what tradition is. If the Arab mentality is too scrupulous to accept a *hadîth* without knowing the chain of its reporters (*isnâd*), still less would its scruples allow it to forge false texts; to pretend the contrary is to admit that there are men who risk damnation by piety. "Woe to them for what their hand has written," says the Koran (*Sûrah* "The Cow" [2]:79). The fact that Muslim traditionalists began very early to denounce certain falsifications only confirms what has just been said.

[10] The shock that the Christian suffers from the Koranic version of Bible stories in no way differs from the shock experienced by the Jew in the face of New Testament quotations from the Prophets, not to mention the strange forgetfulness by Christians of Jewish exegesis, which is nonetheless essential for a proper understanding of the Old Testament and could fill many gaps.

The historical perspective—with all its importance for a certain level of Christian doctrine—is legitimate, however, only insofar as it can be included in Platonic non-historicity. Christian "personalism" comes from the fact of the Incarnation and then from the "bhaktic" character of Christianity, a character that in no way prevents this religion from "containing" metaphysics and *gnosis*, for Christ is "the light of the world"; but *gnosis* is not for everyone, and a religion cannot be metaphysical in its actual form; on the other hand Platonism, which is not a religion, can be so. Christian "historicity", which is linked to Jewish "historicity", thus implies no superiority in comparison with other perspectives—nor any inferiority, as long as the characteristic in question is situated on the level to which it rightfully belongs.

*

* *

Does the object of faith take precedence over faith itself or does faith take precedence over its object? Normally it is the object that has precedence over faith since it is what determines faith and provides it with a sufficient reason; but from a certain point of view and in certain cases, faith can be more important than its content and can "force" the gates of Heaven despite the insufficiency of some immediate objects of belief. Faith includes two "poles", one objective and dogmatic and the other subjective and mystical; the ideal is perfect faith in an orthodox truth. It is the idea that engenders faith, and the quality of the idea determines the quality of the faith; and yet the often paradoxical and unforeseeable play of universal Possibility can allow the predominance of the pole "faith" over the pole "idea", so that the Tibetans have been able to say that a dog's tooth which is mistaken for a relic and becomes the object of a sincere and ardent faith actually begins to shine.[11] There can in fact be a faith which, in its very substance, carries the imprint of a truth that ordinary consciousness is more or less unaware of, provided no intrinsic error compromises the quality of its ardor, which must be of such purity and nobility as will safeguard it from

---

[11] The story is told of Valmiki, who, invoking backwards the divine name of Rama, was saved by his faith. The exaggerated character of this story underlines its intention.

serious errors; such faith is like an "existential" intuition of its "intellectual" object. The possibility of a faith that takes precedence over the "ideological" element and "compels" it, so to speak, to an ultimate surrender of truth presupposes a highly contemplative mentality, already freed from many obstacles; furthermore, if the quality of faith can thus compensate for the precariousness of the idea, this idea must appear like a light, however feeble, and not like a darkness; on this plane there are many imponderables.

It is easy to understand the slight respect shown by *bhaktas*, or by some of them, for "word for word" exactness in belief or worship if one takes into consideration their "subjectivism"—we do not say their "individualism"—which finds all the criteria of "truth" in the intensity of faith and the negation of the ego; it is true that such an attitude is not easy to realize in just any sort of traditional climate, unless—apart from all questions of doctrine—one has in mind those simple souls who practice a touching and efficacious devotion to some pious image and who are to be found *sub omni caelo*. We certainly do not wish to confuse naiveté with intrinsic heresy, even when such heresy is passive, although from the point of view of pure truth every limited concept has a provisional aspect of heresy; all we mean to say here is, not that error as such can be right, but that by virtue of the "exception that proves the rule" there exists a *de facto* supremacy of the magic of the soul over the correctness of the symbol and that account must be taken of this supremacy if one wishes to grasp every aspect of the eternal interchange between man and God. Here we have a possibility that perhaps concerns men themselves less than the manner in which God sees and judges them. It is the whole mystery of the "faith that moves mountains" and "saves", whatever our ignorance. A certain reversal of the normal polarity of faith is moreover to be found in all genuine faith in the sense that the object of faith appears at the outset as a "dead letter"; but in this case precisely the normal relationships of things are not affected, for the symbol to be assimilated retains all its value.

*

* *

Gnosis or the *philosophia perennis* is the connecting link between the different religious languages. The mode of manifestation of *gnosis* is "vertical" and more or less "discontinuous"; it is like fire and not water in the sense that fire breaks forth from the invisible and can disappear into it again,[12] whereas water has a continuous existence; but the sacred Scriptures remain the necessary and unchanging basis, the source of inspiration and the criterion of all *gnosis*.[13] Direct and supra-mental intellection is in reality a "remembering" and not an "acquisition": intelligence in this realm does not take cognizance of something located in principle outside itself, but all possible knowledge is on the contrary contained in the luminous substance of the Intellect—which is identified with the *Logos* by "filiation of essence"— so that the "remembering" is nothing other than an actualization, thanks to an occasional external cause or an internal inspiration, of an eternal potentiality of the intellective substance. Discernment exists only in relation to the relative even if this relative lies beyond creation and at the very level of Being, and this explains why the Intellect has been compared to deep sleep—but a sleep eminently non-passive and supra-conscious—untroubled by dreams; the Intellect coincides in its innermost nature with the very Being of things;[14] and this is why *gnosis* underscores the profound continuity between the diverse forms of consciousness of the absolute.

And why this consciousness, some will ask? Because the truth alone makes free; or, better still, because there is no "why" with regard to the truth, which is our intelligence, our freedom, and our very being; if it is not, we are not.

---

[12] Zen, with its "a-doctrinal" character, is particularly representative of this feature of *gnosis*.

[13] It is said in Judaism that esoterism was revealed by God to Moses in the Tabernacle and then subsequently lost, but that wise men were able to reconstitute it, basing themselves on the *Torah*. Whatever may have been the diverse formulations of Christian *gnosis*, the pneumatological mysteries always find their scriptural basis in the New Testament, notably in the prologue to the Gospel of John and in the talk by night with Nicodemus, and also in the Epistles. With regard to "eternal life", there are certainly no "second class" faithful; however, "in my Father's house are many mansions"; equality before God concerns the "external" fact of salvation and not its possible "internal" modes.

[14] It is in this sense that the Gospel can say of the Word-Light—the divine Intellect—that "all things were made by him; and without him was not anything made that was made" (John 1:3).

Diversity of Revelation

Since there is only one Truth, must we not conclude that there is only one Revelation, one sole Tradition possible? To this we reply, first of all, that Truth and Revelation are not absolutely equivalent terms since Truth is situated beyond forms, whereas Revelation, or the Tradition derived from it, belongs to the formal order, and this indeed by definition; but to speak of form is to speak of diversity, and thus plurality; the grounds for the existence and nature of form are expression, limitation, differentiation. What enters into form thereby enters also into number, hence into repetition and diversity; the formal principle—inspired by the infinity of the divine Possibility—confers diversity on this repetition. One could conceive, it is true, that there might be only one Revelation or Tradition for our human world and that diversity might be realized through other worlds, unknown to man or even unknowable by him; but this would imply a failure to understand that what determines the difference among forms of Truth is the difference among human receptacles. For thousands of years humanity has been divided into several fundamentally different branches constituting as many complete humanities, more or less closed in on themselves; the existence of spiritual receptacles so different and so original demands a differentiated refraction of the one Truth. Let us note that this is not always a question of race, but more often of human groups, very diverse perhaps, but nonetheless subject to mental conditions which, taken as a whole, make of them sufficiently homogeneous spiritual recipients, though this fact does not prevent individuals from being able to leave their frameworks, for the human collectivity never has anything absolute about it. This being so, we can say that the diverse Revelations do not really contradict one another since they do not apply to the same receptacle and since God never addresses the same message to two or more receptacles having a divergent character, that is, corresponding analogically to dimensions that are formally incompatible; a contradiction can arise only between things situated on the same level. The apparent antinomies between Traditions are like differences of language or symbol; contradictions are an aspect of the human receptacles, not of God; diversity in the world is a result of its remoteness from the divine Principle, which amounts to saying that the Creator cannot will both that the world should be and that it should not be the world.

If Revelations more or less exclude one another, this is so of necessity since God, when He speaks, expresses Himself in an absolute mode; but this absoluteness concerns the universal content rather than the form, to which it applies only in a relative and symbolical sense, for the form is a symbol of the content and so too of humanity as a whole, to which precisely this content is addressed. It cannot be that God would compare the diverse Revelations from the outside as might a scholar; He keeps Himself as it were at the center of each Revelation as if it were the only one. Revelation speaks an absolute language because God is absolute, not because the form is absolute; in other words the absoluteness of the Revelation is absolute in itself, but relative in its form.

The language of the sacred Scriptures is divine, but at the same time it is necessarily the language of men; it is thus made for men and could be divine only in an indirect manner. This incommensurability between God and our means of expression appears clearly in the Scriptures, where neither our words nor our logic are adequate to the celestial intention; the language of mortals does not *a priori* envision things *sub specie aeternitatis*. The uncreated Word shatters created speech while directing it toward the Truth; in this way it manifests its transcendence in relation to the limitations of human logic; man must be able to overcome these limits if he wishes to attain the divine meaning of the words, and he overcomes them in metaphysical knowledge, the fruit of pure intellection, and in a certain fashion also in love, when he touches the essences. To wish to reduce divine Truth to the conditionings of earthly truth is to forget that there is no common measure between the finite and the Infinite.

The absoluteness of Revelation demands its unicity; but such unicity cannot be produced on the level of facts to the point of realizing a fact which is unique of its kind, that is, which constitutes on its own what amounts to an entire genus. Reality alone is unique, on whatever level it is considered: God, universal Substance, divine Spirit immanent in this Substance; but there are "relatively unique" facts, such as Revelation, for since all is relative and since even principles must allow for exceptions—at least in appearance—insofar as they enter into contingencies, unicity must be able to occur on the plane of facts; if unique facts did not exist in any fashion, diversity would be absolute, which is a contradiction pure and simple. The two must both be capable of manifesting themselves, unicity as well as diversity; but the two manifestations are necessarily relative, and the one must limit the other. It results from this on the one hand that diversity cannot abolish unity, which is its substance, and on the other hand that unity or unicity must be contradicted by diversity on its own plane of existence; in other words, in every manifestation of unicity a compensatory diversity must be maintained, and indeed a unique fact occurs only in a part and not in the whole of a cosmos. It could be said that a given fact is unique insofar as it represents God for a given environment, but not insofar as it exists; this existence does not abolish the symbol, however, but repeats it outside the framework within which the unique fact occurred, though on the same plane. Existence, which conveys the divine Word, does not abolish the unicity of a given Revelation within its providential field, but it repeats the manifestation of the Word outside this field; it is thus that diversity, without abolishing the metaphysically necessary manifestation of unicity, nonetheless contradicts it outside a particular framework, though on the same level, in order to show in this way that the uncreated and non-manifested Word alone possesses absolute unicity.

If the objection is raised that at the moment when a Revelation occurs it is nonetheless unique for the world, and not for a part of the world alone, we would reply that diversity does not necessarily occur in simultaneity, but extends also to temporal succession, and this is clearly the case when it is a question of Revelations. Moreover, a unicity of fact must not be confused with a unicity of principle; we do not deny the possibility of a fact unique to the world in a certain period, but that of a fact unique in an absolute sense. A fact appearing unique in space is not so in time, and conversely; but even within each of these conditions of existence, it could never be affirmed that a fact is unique of its kind—for it is the genus or quality, not the particularity, which is in question—for we can measure neither time nor space, and still less other modes that elude us.

This whole doctrine is clearly illustrated by the following example: the sun is unique in our solar system, but it is not so in space; we can see other suns since they are located in space as is ours, but we do not see them as suns. The unicity of our sun is belied by the multiplicity of the fixed stars without thereby ceasing to be valid within the system that is ours under Providence; hence the unicity is manifested in the part, not in the totality, which the part nonetheless represents for us; by the divine Will it "is" thus the totality, though only for us and only insofar as our mind, whose scope is likewise willed by God, does not go beyond forms; but even in this case the part "is" totality as far as its spiritual efficacy is concerned.

*
* *

We observe on earth the existence of diverse races, whose differences are "valid" since there are no "false" as opposed to "true" races; we observe as well the existence of multiple languages, and no one thinks of contesting their legitimacy; the same is true for the sciences and arts. Now it would be astonishing if this diversity did not also occur on the religious plane, that is, if the diversity of human receptacles did not involve a diversity of divine contents—from the point of view of form, not of essence. But just as a man appears, within the framework of each race, simply as "man" and not as a "White" or a "Yellow", and just as each language appears in its own sphere as "language" and not as such and such a language among others, so each religion is necessarily "the religion" on its own plane without any comparative relativization, which would be senseless in view of the end to be attained; to speak of "religion" is to speak of "unique religion"; explicitly to practice one religion is implicitly to practice them all.

An idea or enterprise that comes into collision with insurmountable obstacles is contrary to the nature of things; now the ethnic diversity of humanity and the geographical extent of the earth suffice to render highly unlikely the axiom of one unique religion for all and on the contrary highly likely—to say the least—the need for a plurality of religions; in other words the idea of a single religion does not escape contradiction if one takes account of its claims to absoluteness and universality, on the one hand, and the psychological and physical impossibility of their realization, on the other, not to mention the antinomy between such claims and the necessarily relative character of all religious mythology; only pure metaphysics and pure prayer are absolute and therefore universal. As for "mythology", it is indispensable—apart from its intrinsic content of truth and efficacy—for enabling metaphysical and essential truth to "gain a footing" in a given human collectivity.

Religion is a "supernaturally natural" fact, which proves its truth—from the point of view of extrinsic proofs—by its human universality, so that the plurality and ubiquity of the religious phenomenon constitute a powerful argument in favor of religion as such. Just as a plant makes no mistake in turning toward the light, so man makes no mistake in following Revelation and therefore Tradition. There is something infallible in the natural instinct of animals and also in the "supernatural instinct" of men; but man is the only "animal" capable of going against nature as such, whether wrongly by violating it or else by transcending it.

Is There a Natural Mysticism?

The concept of a "natural mysticism" amounts to a begging of the question that permits one to classify, once and for all, forms of spirituality that do not enter into the framework of a given religion, which is held to be the sole true and supernatural religion: it is then maintained that a spirituality located outside this framework, though it may seem to be on the highest level, remains in fact enclosed within the created, of which it will perhaps attain the center or summit, but which it can in no way transcend since man can do nothing without God and since, precisely, God intervenes directly only in the one existing supernatural religion and not outside it; one will readily admit that supernatural graces could be bestowed on some non-Christian saint,[1] but these graces will be held to have an "irregular" and quasi-accidental character and to be produced not as a result of this saint's religion but despite it.

The principal objection to this view is that the "created" is not absolutely—nor in every respect—"created", or in other words that there cannot be an absolute relativity,[2] for otherwise the created would not be distinct from nothingness, which amounts to saying in ordinary language that it would be nonexistent; the "uncreated" or the "supernatural" is thus concealed within the "created", the "natural", and can be attained in principle by the Intellect, which itself includes essentially a "supernatural" or "uncreated" element. If the supernatural is within things by virtue of their very Existence, it is by the Intellect that it can be actualized, so that the two supernatural poles of creation are pure Existence and pure Intellect; the supernatural is essentially "Being" and "Intelligence" or "Reality" and "Consciousness". Now the anti-metaphysical and purely "phenomenalist" character of the thesis

---

[1] As it happens the concept "natural mysticism" saw the light of day in the Christian world, although logically it could serve the cause of no matter what dogmatism.

[2] There can be a relative absoluteness, as we have explained elsewhere, and this asymmetry shows precisely that the absolute and the real coincide. The possibility of reality does not entail that of an absolutely real relativity, hence the absolute reality of relativity as such.

of "natural mysticism" appears above all in the denial of the metaphysical transparency of things or in the prejudice that considers creatures only in relation to their separative "projection".

It is important to specify here that the supernatural or the divine is quite evidently not "contained" within the created or the world, despite certain appearances, but that it is in principle accessible starting from its cosmic traces, which is quite different; this means that things, thanks to their Existence, and the intellective subject, thanks to Knowledge, open concrete ways to the Absolute. There is no question here of either "pantheism" or "panentheism", for we are not saying that the world as such is God or that it contains God, but simply that the world, insofar as it exists—or insofar as it is not nonexistent—is an aspect of its divine Cause, hence "something of God"; the Divinity, while being absolutely transcendent in relation to the world, is nonetheless "present" at the center of all cosmic reality. The world shows its "divine quality" in two ways: first by the miracle of its Existence, as we have just said, and second—on the basis or within the framework of this existential miracle—by its multiple and inexhaustible symbolism, which manifests the Infinite in the most diverse ways. Likewise the Intellect "is divine": first because it is a knower—or because it is not a non-knower—and second because it reduces all phenomena to their Principle, seeing the Cause in every effect and thus surmounting at a certain level the vertiginous and devouring multiplicity of the phenomenal world. When we say that the Intellect "is not a non-knower" or that the world "is not nonexistent", we are expressing a shade of meaning that is far from insignificant, for the negative expression here comes much closer than the positive to firmly grasping the necessity or self-evidence of the matter in question.

Existence crystallizes, divides, and disperses; Intelligence on the contrary brings back to unity; however, if subjects—human, animal, angelic, or others—are nonetheless multiple, it is precisely because they are in Existence and because, by reason of this fact, the existential principle renders them diverse; conversely, if universal Existence is one, this is because it proceeds from the divine Intellect, manifesting it in a crystallizing mode without thereby losing its metaphysical homogeneity. Once a thing exists there is within it "all that exists", hence Existence and, in fact, absolute Reality, of which Existence is only the "illusory dimension" advancing into "nothingness"; in the same way there is in every act of knowledge "all that knows", hence the Principle of all possible knowledge, namely, the divine Subject or Self; but this Subject is in itself beyond the polarization into subject and object.

In order to avoid all misunderstanding, it must be emphasized that there is no question here of any naturalism: we are not saying either that the Intellect suffices in fact for salvation or that it can be wholly effective in the absence of a traditional wisdom; what must be said is that the Intellect, once it is "deployed" by virtue of a pre-existing wisdom, suffices for knowing what salvation consists in and what its conditions are; once actualized the Intellect carries its criteria within itself. The "subjective supernatural" has need—"accidentally" and not "essentially"—of the "objective supernatural", but once it is thus "awakened to itself" by what corresponds to it outside of us, no extrinsic objection can concern it further. It is sometimes said that there is no proof of the validity of the Intellect; this is a contradiction in terms, for the fact that such a proof cannot be furnished to meet a particular artificial mental need or that possible proofs are inaccessible to a given intelligence in no way invalidates the self-evidence of truth, any more than the eventual impossibility of proving to the mad that we are sane and they are not removes anything from the objective fact of our sanity or the consciousness we have of it; and if, according to an argument as facile as it is absurd, everything in the intelligence, even mathematical evidence, might be illusion, the same hypothesis can be applied as well and *a fortiori* to the external or objective proofs of a conviction. If everything in pure intelligence could be delusion, everything in phenomena could be so as well with still less improbability, for phenomena are made for intelligence and not the reverse; miracles are not done for animals. But in reality both hypotheses are absurd since intelligence and intelligibility exist; if there is intelligence there must be something intelligible, and if there is something to understand there must be a mind to understand it. There can be false phenomena, false miracles for example, but there cannot be evidence that is intellective yet false, whether it is a question of mathematics or metaphysics; an oasis can be a mirage, but two and two cannot make other than four anymore than the world can be deprived of a transcendent cause. To claim, for the sake of furthering some argument or other, that one of the poles of the Universe, intellectual or existential, is illusory on its own plane—for all is illusory in relation to the eternal actuality of God—annuls at the same time the respective complementary pole and ends logically in complete nihilism.

Be that as it may, we must distinguish between a perspective that is intellectual and unitive and another that is existential and separative: the first envisions everything in relation to unity, even Existence ("all is *Âtmâ*"), whereas the second sees everything in relation to separativity, even Intelligence ("the intellect does not reach beyond the created"); this second perspective is in fact "cosmocentric" and "phenomenalist", not theocentric and metaphysical. According to this second view, the world is comparable to concentric circles which, while reflecting the center, never attain it, so that there is absolute separation; according to the first perspective, on the contrary, the world is like a star, every ray of which unites the periphery to the central point; and this perspective, which is that of "metaphysical transparency" or "essential identity", sees God in everything that exists and "sees" Him or "realizes" Him in a certain manner in the impersonal and universal mystery of the Intellect. Now it is a matter of combining these two modes of vision, for each is valid in its own way; it is certain that things—as such—are infinitely separated from the Principle and that there is therefore no possible continuity between it and them, but it is just as true in another respect that things—by virtue of their essential reality, that is, their pure existence and their immediate symbolism—"are not other than the Principle", if one may so express it, for otherwise they would be either a second Absolute or a nothingness pure and simple. If we combine the image of the concentric circles with that of the star, we obtain the spider's web, which is a particularly intelligible symbol of the cosmos; the concentric circles could also be replaced by the spiral which, ending as it does in the center, thus marks the "divine continuity" of the cosmos; or again the center of the star could be removed so as to have rays converging on a luminous void, thus marking the infinity of the divine Center.

With all these images, which despite their apparent simplicity verge upon the limit of what is humanly expressible, we wish to convey the idea that the "supernatural" resides above all in the nature of things and not in an essential or exclusive way—such as a *deus ex machina*—in some condition belonging to the phenomenal order. Such conditions can certainly attach themselves to the existential and intellective supernatural and thus can permit the actualization of a spiritual virtuality, but their relatively circumstantial function excludes precisely the possibility of a complete monopoly of the supernatural; in other words, if the supernatural already resides in the metaphysical structure of the created, without for all that being reducible to the "natural" world, this implies that it has a character of universality and for this reason that it cannot but offer itself to man in one form or another wherever it meets with the necessary receptivity; now this receptivity with regard to the supernatural is proved by the existence of a corresponding wisdom in most of those cases where prejudice would like to see only a "natural mysticism". It is true that an apparently rational and practically anthropocentric aspect of Shankarian Vedantism or of the Buddhist *Dhamma* is liable to convey the impression of a purely human wisdom, but this is simply a question of external dialectic and technical opportuneness, not mental limitation; this is proven on the one hand by the transcendent character of these doctrines envisioned in their totality and on the other hand by the fact that they are always accompanied by initiations, which are themselves supernatural by definition, this characteristic constituting their sufficient reason; from another angle spiritual currents such as Vishnuism and Amidism are ways of grace or mercy and as such do not have any rationalizing aspect, at least no more than is found in Christianity.

Some will be of the opinion perhaps that the phrase "natural mysticism" is nevertheless not devoid of meaning; in fact it is not possible that a mysticism situated entirely on the human plane should not occur somewhere, since confusions are within the possibility of man. But then it will be a false mysticism, so that the phrase "natural mysticism" constitutes either an error or an abuse of language; it is a false "mysticism" which is unaware of the supernatural, whether by denying it or by wrongly claiming it for itself, and which remains in this way cut off from all "mystery". The sacred and age-old traditions of the East are there to demonstrate that this could never be the case for a wisdom which, being a receptacle of divine life, cannot lack the corresponding content and that in this realm more than in any other the Spirit "bloweth where it listeth".

*

*   *

The great contradiction between the postulate of a "natural mysticism"[3] and its complement, the Judeo-Christian concept of the

---

[3] Or "natural religion", which amounts to the same thing, taken as a whole.

"supernatural", results from the fact that the terms of this distinction are applied in a way that is counter to the nature of things: in the one case a particular form of wisdom is labeled "natural" even though it transcends essentially all that is "nature", whereas in the other case factors are included in the "supernatural" that in no way go beyond the realm of phenomena; it even seems that a given foreign wisdom is blamed for not being equally enclosed, or rather one does not see in the fact that it is not so enclosed anything but a disappointing lack of realism, even a lack of sincerity; speculations that have been developed to the limit of the expressible are described as "dreams in the abstract", as if such an assessment were not, to say the least, a confession of metaphysical incompetence. There is always the same reversal of normal relationships: the "phenomenal" element plays in practice the role of a *deus ex machina* to the detriment of a given principial, hence supra-phenomenal, truth and a given effective knowledge of the same order; a *petitio principii* is substituted for what is self-evident and thereby also for the imprescriptible rights of what constitutes our very Essence. But since a verbal fiction does not suffice to change the nature of things, the falseness of the postulate in question is fatally betrayed by the "fissures" of a logic that aims at being impeccable and disinterested, but whose processes of "objective analysis" are illusions at least as pernicious as those one expects to uncover in a hypothetical "natural mysticism".

The differences between traditional forms translate what constitutes the sufficient reason of each; but for those who seek to resolve every difficulty by the hypothesis of a "natural" mysticism or religion, these differences can do no more than indicate so many deviations from the one unique religion or so many different ways of placing oneself outside the only accepted "supernatural". Without asking oneself, for example, what impression the Song of Songs[4] might make on a Buddhist monk, the Mahayanic *sûtras* are taken for poetic artifices, as if there could be effects without a cause, that is, as if the spiritual and moral force of the "Great Vehicle", its extraordinary vitality and

---

[4] Is this "oriental poem", which Saint Bernard and others have taken the trouble to commentate, less strange in its literalness than the *Sukhâvatî-Vyûhas*, leaving aside any question of taste?

the profundity of its art, could be explained as arising from fantasies of the imagination[5]—or as if the immensity of the result in space and time, affecting societies, cultures, and souls, did not reflect the greatness and the quality of absoluteness in the prime mover.

Another example of the "optical illusion" in question is the following: some people think that the ineluctability of the law of *karma* annuls, logically, the merciful power of Amitabha; but predestination, which no theologian can deny in full awareness of the facts unless he also denies that God "knew" the destiny of every creature even "before" the creation, is opposed just as much—or as little—to the redeeming power of Christ. Or again: it is recognized that in Buddhism *Nirvâna* comes before the Buddha, so that the latter is like an expression of the former—an expression which, as such, is "illusory"— whereas in the Judeo-Christian perspective God on the contrary comes before Paradise, which means that Paradise is reducible in a certain way to God; the second point of view could certainly be regarded as more "supernatural",[6] but the refusal to admit or understand the first, were one even to study it, has at root a very "natural" explanation, namely, an anti-metaphysical horror of "nothingness" and a desire never to lose contact with the human[7]—to install the human and the individual even within the Divine and to place the Absolute in a sublimated

---

[5] When these Scriptures are criticized for their legendary character while the strict historicity of the Gospels is emphasized, a most important criterion is forgotten, namely, the efficacy of a sacred text; if this efficacy is guaranteed for a naturally contemplative and symbolist mentality by a more or less mythological form, of what use is a historicity this mentality does not require? In the same line of thought it may be noted that it is in the nature of esoterism to base itself outwardly on a precarious and often almost imperceptible element, to announce itself as if in passing, and this explains how it is that the last sermons of the Buddha—the authenticity of which is sometimes questioned—were unfolded as it were "on the margin" of the great exoteric teaching. The basis for Hesychasm in the New Testament—to add this one example—has the same character of precariousness.

[6] Needless to say we have no "preference" for one or the other since each is legitimate from its own point of view and since they are qualitatively equivalent.

[7] An "optical illusion" of this kind is produced in a certain Hindu bhaktism that readily postulates a supreme spiritual experience situated beyond all, even non-

human dimension. The absoluteness of man and of history entails the humanity and historicity of the Absolute, and conversely.

Another argument that is far from being negligible is that of miracles: why does God allow miracles if not in order to say something? We are not thinking here, of course, of the prodigies with which legend loves to adorn the memory of saints, but of the signs—supernatural in character because they have a divine cause, even though they are obviously produced within nature—by which God favors His elect or some among them; an apparently miraculous fact certainly proves nothing in itself, but it proves everything when it can be placed positively in connection with a traditional spirituality and is accompanied by criteria guaranteeing its authenticity. Whatever may be the gulf that separates one religious language from another, these signs are often the same: thus the contemporaries of Honen Shonin, the most illustrious representative of Japanese Amidism, observed in their master the same phenomena of luminosity—including reading at night with neither light nor candle—as the contemporaries of the great Teresa were to observe of their saint some centuries later; or again this same Honen had visions, shared sometimes by those around him, of Buddhas and *Bodhisattvas*, just as our mystics of the West have been able to behold Christ and the Virgin: in each case there is the same clarity of vision and the same effusion of graces. It would be pointless to enumerate all the miraculous facts—healings, phenomena of levitation, of bilocation, and so on—by which God, whatever the metaphysical conception with which He is clothed in a particular Revelation, corroborates both His truth and the sanctity flowing from it, with the manifest effect of confirming the faithful in their faith;

---

formal, knowledge, which amounts to saying that there could be an experience that would in no sense be knowledge. In a similar way this same "mytho-theology" speaks of a divine personal "form" manifesting beyond the non-formal divine Reality, which simply proves that this perspective confuses the non-formal, which eminently embraces all "form", with the amorphous or that it confuses the non-differentiated Consciousness (*prajnâ*) of the Self with the "dark night" of "extinction". The very human desire to be thus placed at the summit seems rather characteristic of the perspectives of love, although it ill accords with their climate of "humility"; the same objection does not arise, however, in relation to the sapiential perspectives, for the hierarchy of values exists, being independent of our desires and choices.

what we would underscore here is quite simply that the similarity and the number of miracles in all the different religions are too great not to have significance, and they preclude in any case the possibility that miracles might be true on one side and false on the other, unless one wishes to reduce the human condition to absurdity.

Vicissitudes of Spiritual Temperaments

Human nature is made in such a way that it tends to lock itself into some limitation, and this tendency can only be accentuated in an age that is everywhere engaged in destroying the frameworks of universality. Starting from the distinction "love-knowledge"—or *bhakti-jnâna*—we can say that the *bhakta*, the volitive and affective spirit, whose perspective is based mainly on the alternative "charity-egoism", risks neglecting "objective truth", whereas the *jnânin*, the intellective spirit, who on the contrary sees things in terms of the alternative "truth-error", is exposed to the temptation of neglecting the strictly human perfections and perhaps even the human link with God. We are thinking here above all of "spiritual types" and not their corresponding realizations, especially as regards the *jnânin*, who may indeed be somewhat lacking in "charity" insofar as he is an "intellectual genius"—or insofar as he is induced in practice to shut himself up in theory alone even while of necessity recognizing its limitations—but not insofar as he is a "realized" or "delivered spirit";[1] on the other hand *bhakti*, which comprises more "elementary" and "easier" realizations—because they do not necessarily go beyond the human plane—is conceivable apart from intellectuality properly so called and even, although doubtless only in a partial way, apart from strict orthodoxy. A bhaktic perfection from which the "intellectual" element is lacking—in one form or another—is like a body without a skeleton, since it is situated outside its normal and necessary setting, a traditional civilization; this setting functions precisely as an "outward skeleton" for the *bhakta*: it is the tradition that "thinks" for him and neutralizes the more or less inevitable "extravagances" of the bhaktic devotee; we can sacrifice our judgment—as obedience sometimes demands—but only on condition of being certain that this judgment or intelligence exists around us in the traditional environment. In an inversely analogous way, a jnanic perfection from which the element "charity" is lacking or which some

---

[1] Strictly speaking, it is only in the latter case that the term *jnânin* is applicable. Let us add that we are as always using the word "intellectual" in its strictest sense, which refers to the Intellect and therefore does not concern the purely "mental" speculations of logicians.

concession to mental passion deprives of the serenity connatural with contemplation is like a skeleton without flesh: here it is beauty of soul which provides the normal "environment" or "climate" or which is the complement, not of intellection as such, but of the mental activity resulting from it; this beauty, composed of peace and generosity—but not of vagueness or laxity!—is inherent in *jnâna* to the extent it can be identified with pure *gnosis*.

One sees from this confrontation that the condition of equilibrium or integrality is "outward" while at the same time being indirectly "intellectual" with the volitive man and that it is "inward" while at the same time being apparently "moral" with the intellective man; we say "indirectly" because the traditional surroundings assert themselves above all through symbolism and "apparently" because the charity of the *jnânin* is not so much an individual or psychological attitude as an impersonal conformity to what "pre-exists" *in divinis*. *Bhakti* is still situated *a priori* and as a way on the human plane, whereas *jnâna*—or the Intellect, which is at the same time both its "seat" and "organ"—lies beyond the ego; hence the distinctive "quality" of the *jnânin* is not strictly human, for it does not properly belong to any individual: it is the Spirit that "bloweth where it listeth" and of which one does not know "whence it cometh, and whither it goeth".[2]

---

[2] As Coomaraswamy has pointed out with a truly Hindu boldness, "There always remains a last step, in which the ritual is abandoned and the relative truths of theology are denied. As it was by the knowledge of good and evil that man fell from his first estate, so it must be from the knowledge of good and evil, from the moral law, that he must be delivered at last. However far one may have gone, there remains a last step to be taken, involving a dissolution of all former values. A church or society—the Hindu would make no distinction—that does not provide a way of escape from its own regimen, and will not let its people go, is defeating its own ultimate purpose" (*Hinduism* and *Buddhism*, Part I, "The Social Order"). It is not a question here exclusively of *jnâna*, but of a reality that is in any case nearer to *jnâna* than to *bhakti*. Let us add that the freedom of being outside forms can be quite interior and is necessarily so, to a greater or lesser degree, in the religions of Semitic origin, where spirituality takes a social form and where the part is thereby indissolubly connected with the whole; but even here there are cases of passing beyond all form: Mary Magdalene, the anchorite Paul, Mary of Egypt, and others lived without sacraments for many years while being already saints. All the same, since it is necessary to transcend forms "from above" and not "from below", the principle in question could not furnish the least pretext for ease, to say nothing of an arbitrary and individualistic rejection of dogmas

Nevertheless, for the jnanic contemplative as well there must be something that performs the function of an outward and symbolist framework, just as for the *bhakta* there must be something that corresponds to the "inward environment" of the *jnânin*: this outward framework of the *jnânin* will be beauty in its aspect of intelligibility, of symbolism "lived", or of harmony, and not in its aspect of superficial attractiveness; it is beauty which, without being actually indispensable, nonetheless constitutes the natural and providential complement of intellective concentration—"abstract" in a certain relative sense—hence an indirect element of equilibrium; it is like a perfume of truth, allowing the intelligence to come to rest without mistrust. And it is not without reason that the beauty in question should be the beauty of virgin nature rather than of temples: for nature reflects something spontaneous and unlimited, something also timeless, which fully corresponds to the altogether primordial freedom of the pure Intellect; the spirit of the *jnânin* is indeed "anterior" to all crystallization, being everywhere and nowhere.[3] As for *bhakti*, the "inward environment" it requires is none other than intelligence—not such as constitutes the qualification for *gnosis*, of course, but discernment on the phenomenal and rational plane; one is reminded that Saint Teresa of Avila never accepted that nuns need be stupid. What matters in the first place for the *bhakta* is perfection of will and not of intelligence, hence his ten-

and rites. Hermits and wandering pilgrims constitute an essential aspect of the Church—every Church—and their disappearance, in no matter what civilization, is a calamity having incalculable effects; contrary to popular prejudice nothing is less "useless" to society than the compensatory and purifying presence of those who are "dead in this life". Whether one likes it or not, there are spiritual modes that do not admit of being "recruited" any more than the wind that "bloweth where it listeth". The fact that a man can in principle "die to himself" under any circumstances, hence also in the world, by no means implies that he can always do so in fact nor that the vocations of silence or solitude do not preserve all their rights, without which monasticism itself could not be justified.

[3] It is sometimes said that the ancient hermits, notably the Desert Fathers, used to seek out the most "desolate" places in nature, and this is thought to provide an argument against an "aestheticism" that is by no means in question; it is forgotten that these "desolate" places are neither factory walls nor office furnishings and that it is actually impossible for them to be outside the framework of beauty, for the simple reason that in virgin nature beauty is everywhere, in harshness as in gentleness. The non-formal must never be confused with the formless nor above all with the trivial.

dency to underestimate the intelligence, as if volitive perfection could dispense with the truth that determines the direction and modes of the will.

All these considerations can be summed up as follows: if we see in *jnâna* a "virile" way and in *bhakti* a "feminine" way,[4] we could say that this virility requires an extrinsic feminine complement, or even a double complement, one "inward" and moral and another "outward" and aesthetic, and that bhaktic femininity requires in its turn a double virile complement, one outward and traditional and another inward and mental; in other words love needs a complement of intelligence or discernment in its traditional surroundings and possibly also in the soul, according to the level of the way, whereas intellectual activity needs a complement of beauty in the soul and secondarily in the visible environment. It is necessary to avoid mental disquiet, its unconscious "egoism" and its sclerosis, as well as an opaque sentimentalism, which believes that by some virtue or other it can make up for absence of truth.

Before going further it is perhaps useful to specify once again that intellectual genius should not be confused with the mental acuity of logicians: intellectual intuition comprises in its essence a contemplativity that is in no way part of the rational capacity, this capacity being logical rather than contemplative; now it is contemplative power, receptivity toward the uncreated Light, the opening of the Eye of the heart, which distinguishes transcendent intelligence from reason. Reason perceives the general and proceeds by logical operations, whereas Intellect perceives the principial—the metaphysical—and proceeds by intuition; intellection is concrete in relation to rational abstractions and abstract in relation to divine Concreteness; from another point of view we are tempted to say that logic is to intellectual intuition what this intuition is to effective *gnosis*, although the terms in question are not strictly comparable. "Genius" is not in the Intellect as such but in the receptacle: it is a "supernaturally natural" cleft in human opacity.

Now one might ask oneself why the soul of the intellective needs to concern itself with charity, at least—or above all—in conditions so

---

[4] On the other hand *bhakti* includes an aspect of virility or resolution on the plane of the will, and *jnâna* an aspect of femininity or receptivity on the plane of the Intellect.

abnormal as to deprive it of a traditional moral culture, while at the same time obliging it to put the emphasis on theory; to this we would reply that the relationship between knowledge and virtue, which is clearly indirect, does not signify that the Intellect is insufficient and has need of extrinsic help, but rather that man is not the Intellect and that an absence of virtue can lead in one degree or another to a split between man and his intelligence: man can be the infallible mouthpiece of the Spirit, but the relationship between the one and the other is a grace, except where the "Self" has absorbed the "I" to the point of leaving nothing but a transparent screen. Apart from this sublime station, it avails a man nothing to be infallible on some given plane, his infallibility providing no security pact between him and God; his intelligence can be darkened, or rather it can withdraw, and then it is the man and not intelligence that is darkened; the mind can wear itself out when the soul neglects to "repose in God", but the Intellect remains intact. Metaphysics is beyond charity, it is true, but a metaphysician without charity seriously risks compromising the doctrine because of the indirect repercussions of this defect upon his operative intelligence. According to a very wise remark of Saint Teresa of the Child Jesus—a remark we have had occasion to quote elsewhere—Saint Peter would not have denied Christ if, instead of relying on his own strength in asserting that he would never deny him, he had added: "with thy help", hence "with the help of God". Indeed the danger for the intelligence, whether ordinary or superior—though in the latter case it is its "non-divine face" alone that is in question—is to place too much trust not in its light as such, which is normal, but in the presence of that light; this presence depends on grace, as we have said, for no man has the power to create his own spirit. Be that as it may, it is important to know how to combine antinomical truths: what we mean to say is that the Intellect possesses not only the aspect of a "gift", but also that of a "personal essence"; the second aspect neutralizes the first in proportion to the power or "actualization" of the intellective grace. In short, if a man can "have" the Truth, he can also "be" it.

An objection might here be raised that charity needs to be transcended in *gnosis* and that it is illogical to concern oneself with it since knowledge, being beyond oppositions, contains the undifferentiated quintessence of every virtue; to this the reply must be made that positive charity is necessary to the extent the individual has not understood the meaning of negative virtue; indeed the *jnânin* does not ask,

"Am I charitable?" but, "Is this being free of egoism?", which means that his virtue is negative just as his theosophy[5] is apophatic. Intrinsic virtue lies beyond all moral specification; it is our fundamental being, such that to be virtuous means to abstain from the vices of fallen nature, which by no means prevents this abstention from being able to assume, according to circumstances, an aspect of volitive affirmation, hence of exteriorization and activity. On the other hand the specifically moral perspective, which the *jnânin* or "gnostic" must transcend, implies adding works and virtues to our being, and it thereby tends toward individualism; in practice it runs the risk of putting works and virtues in place of God, whereas the jnanic perspective, which confines itself to maintaining the soul in the virginity of our fundamental being, is impersonal from the fact that it sees virtue, not in human initiatives, but in an existential quality, namely, the primordial and innocent nature of creation; but this fundamental being, or theomorphic nature, is an ontological layer deeper than the level of the fall. Virtue is not thereby dissociated from contemplation, but rests so to speak in God; it is less a will to do than a consciousness of being, and this is why it withdraws from the plane of moral oppositions instead of entering actively into their play. But transcending the virtues could not in any case be equivalent to an absence of the virtues; on the contrary, it is freedom from individual limitations, which the divine Qualities assume in the human ego;[6] what counts most for God is the quality

---

[5] Theosophy in the proper sense of the word, of course, and not some form of neo-spiritualism. Theosophy, which is none other than doctrinal *gnosis*, is distinguished from theology by the fact that it has a sapiential essence and has no call to concern itself with the question of what is opportune.

[6] The irreversible relationship between "good" and "being"—the first reducible to the second and therein finding its essence, but the second independent and transcendent in relation to the first—is indicated by the term *sattva*, which designates the ascending cosmic tendency, hence also the "good" as such, and which refers etymologically to *Sat*, "Being". "He only *is* free from virtues and vices and all their fatal consequences who never became anyone; he only *can* be free who is no longer anyone; impossible to be freed from oneself and also to remain oneself. The liberation from good and evil that seemed impossible and is impossible for the man whom we define by what he does or thinks and who answers the question 'Who is that?', 'It's me', is possible only for him who can answer at the Sundoor to the question 'Who art thou?', 'Thyself'" (Ananda K. Coomaraswamy, *Hinduism and Buddhism*, Part I, "Theology and Autology").

of our contemplation, for to be contemplated is for God a manner of "being", if one may so express it, in the sense that the fact of human contemplation is a consequence of divine "being".

*
*   *

The bhaktic spirit distinguishes *a priori* between God and the ego, between "other" and "I". The "other" fulfills in practice the role of God in the sense of the familiar Gospel teaching;[7] but the ego will denote for the *bhakta*—at least in neo-bhaktism—the quintessence of all evil, to the extent of replacing the devil, as if the latter had ceased to exist outside us; it is true that the dangers of such a simplification are counterbalanced by the traditional quality of the environment, but this safeguard obviously collapses as soon as one leaves those surroundings. The reduction of the devil to the ego amounts in practice to the devil's abolition and thus to forgetfulness concerning the powers of illusion; the door then stands open to a puerile optimism, which is all the more dangerous in that it is mingled unsuspectingly with progressivist optimism and accepts everything the modern world contains in the way of trivialization and falsification. Moreover a too exclusive—and in any case inconsistent—"satanization" of the ego entails a too simplistic "divinization" of the "other", which means that replacing the devil by the "I" goes hand in hand with replacing God by the "neighbor", whence an "altruism" that appears as an end in itself and thus loses all contact with metaphysical truth, and so with genuine spirituality.[8] In such a perspective the distinction, essential

---

[7] In Christian language one speaks of "pride" rather than of "ego". Let us add that both Catholic and Orthodox *bhakta*s are protected by dogma, which is scarcely the case for the Hindu *bhakta*, who is on the one hand more "universalist" than the Christian, but on the other more vulnerable, at least in our time. "Narrowness" is sometimes a protection; "breadth" is admirable only when one is capable of supporting it. The classical *bhakti* of India was very narrow in relation to *jnâna*; it was Ramakrishna, it seems to us, who "broadened" it, he who was at the same time *bhakta* and *jnânin*, which in no way means that every *bhakta* must or can follow his example.

[8] "In the [Buddhist] saying, 'For one who has attained, there is naught dearer than Self', we recognize the doctrine of the Upanishads that the 'Self alone is truly dear', the Hermetic 'Love thy Self', and the Christian doctrine that 'A man,

though it is, between truth and error is obliterated: it is the ego as such that alone is "error", and it is God and the neighbor that alone are "truth"; there is then nothing wrong in believing that two and two make five, provided one "does good" or "renders service". But since it is never possible to hold in a completely consistent way that error is "I", one is forced to exclude from egoity particular manifestations of the ego, thus adding to the ego yet one more illusion; similarly, since it is impossible to admit without contradiction that truth is the "other", one inevitably ends by confusing the notions of truth and God, which moreover is in complete accordance with a contempt—dressed up as humility—for the intelligence; from here it is but a step to acceptance of the Antichrist out of humility or charity, even for the sake of being "nice". In a general way *bkaktas* have a certain interest in depreciating the intelligence: "intellectual pride"—or what is believed to be such—is rejected, only to be replaced by a pride toward the Intellect, as if this second pride were preferable to the first, and so one slips into the "sin against the Holy Spirit".

The two positions of which we have just spoken above—locating the devil in the ego and God in the neighbor—are nonetheless perfectly well founded provided they are kept within their indispensable context: they are valid, that is to say, only in a certain respect and not in any other, or more precisely they are imperative on the moral plane and as a remedy against our natural egoism, but not outside the polarity *ego-alter* and the problem of egoity. The intelligence that distinguishes us from animals is a gift of God in the same way as is

---

out of charity, ought to love himself [for the sake of salvation] more than he loves any other person' [Saint Thomas Aquinas, *Summa Theologica*, II-II, 26, 4], that is, that Self for whose sake he must deny himself" (Ananda K. Coomaraswamy, *Hinduism and Buddhism*, Part II, "The Doctrine"). But with regard to the individuality we shall be able to say, "Such an one no longer loves himself or others, but is the Self in himself and in them. Death to one's self is death to 'others'; and if the 'dead man' seems to be 'unselfish', this will not be the result of altruistic motives, but accidentally, and because he is literally un-self-ish. Liberated from himself, from all status, all duties, all rights, he has become a Mover-at-will (*kâmachârî*), like the Spirit (*Vâyu, âtmâ devânâm*) that 'moveth as it will' (*yathâ vasham charati*), and as Saint Paul expresses it, 'no longer under the law'"(*Hinduism and Buddhism*, Part I, "Theology and Autology"). "The mere presence of these men in a society to which they no longer belong, by its affirmation of ultimate values, affects all values. . . . Blessed is the man on whose tomb can be written, *Hic jacet nemo*" (*Hinduism and Buddhism*, Part I, "The Social Order").

charity, and the latter is not even possible without the former; it is not enough to be "harmless as doves"; it is also necessary to be "wise as serpents": against the exclusiveness of a moral and "subjectivist" idealism—an exclusiveness that is impracticable in a world that is breaking down—it is necessary to maintain the "discerning of spirits" in the very interest of the idealism in question, for this idealism is necessary to us from a certain point of view, but not from every point of view. When it is taken in isolation, moral subjectivism—with the sentimentality implied by the extent of this artificial isolation—has something "feminine" about it; now integral femininity corresponds to a "part" and not a "totality",[9] so that the feminization of spirituality can only mark a disequilibrium and a movement toward dissolution; it is the substitution of "colors" for "forms" or of "sounds" for "rhythms". That femininity is a necessary element in all spirituality,[10] we would not think of contesting, but one must know how to put each thing in its place.

The question of "altruism" calls for the insertion here of a few remarks on secular and anti-traditional "humanitarianism", which an unreflecting sentimentality too easily confuses with the charity of saints. This "humanitarianism" in fact puts itself forward as a philosophy founded on the idea that man is good; but to believe that man is good is almost always to believe that God is bad, or that He would be bad "if He existed"; and as modern men believe less and less in God—apart from a totally inoperative scientific "deism"—they pour out over God's representatives the resentment they would like to show against God Himself: man is good, they think, but religions are bad; priests, who have invented religions in order to bolster up their own interests and perpetuate their privileges, are bad, and so on. It is the

---

[9] The egalitarianism that has resulted—by deviation and under modern influence—from the bhaktic refusal to make distinctions that are more or less "passional", or presumed to be such, has given rise to a "feminism" hardly compatible with *bhakti*. Feminism, far from being able to confer on woman "rights" that are nonexistent because contrary to the nature of things, can only remove from her her specific dignity; this is the abolition of the eternal-feminine, of the glory woman derives from her celestial prototype. Moreover, the revolt against man—like the cult of youth or contempt of intelligence—is indirectly a revolt against God.

[10] As is proved—if proof were needed—by the mystical role of the Virgin-Mother.

41

satanic inversion of the traditional axiom that God is good and man is bad: God can be called "good" because all possible goodness is derived from Him and every quality expresses His Essence—in a manner that is "indirectly direct"—and not only such and such a function; and man is bad because his will no longer conforms to the profound nature of things, hence to divine "Being", and his false "instinct of self-preservation" makes itself the advocate of every passion and every terrestrial illusion.[11] Many men are good only "by accident", that is, in the absence of circumstances that might actualize in them all the baseness, ferocity, and perfidy of which human nature is capable; it is true that there exists in every man a deeper layer, "pre-satanic" one might say, and this layer is good, but it finds itself buried precisely under the "frozen" crust produced by the "fall" and now become second nature. Only the love of God—or *gnosis*—can break or melt this ice; as for a deliberately "human" virtue, one imputed solely to the resources of our corrupted nature, this is merely a defiance hurled at God; it tries to show fundamentally that man is better than God or that man alone is good—man "despiritualized" and thereby "dehumanized". In reality the busy activity of mankind is a very small thing: man can neither create good nor destroy evil; he can do no more in the long run than cause the bad and the good to change places; and when he does so in the name of an atheistic and demagogic Prometheanism, he ends only in destroying values higher than those he is capable of aiming at and in engendering evils greater than those that he sets out to overcome.[12]

---

[11] Let us recall here that the negative aspects of God are extrinsic and are derived from relativity, that is, from the remoteness of the world from the Principle; this remoteness—or the world, which amounts to the same thing—is derived in its turn from the divine Infinity, which calls for the "illusorily real" possibility of its own negation. We are here touching the boundary of the inexpressible.

[12] How self-defeating are the aims of humanitarianism is to be observed in the fact that it accepts what is most inhuman, namely, mechanization, which suppresses artisanship, hence one of the conditions of human happiness; there was much merit in Gandhi's campaign against the machine, and consequently on behalf of human dignity. Humanitarianism pretends to seek the good of man, but it is blind to things that deserve the name "atrocities" from the spiritual and even simply human point of view, such as the trivialities of advertisements and so forth that infest modern life, causing damage in quite another way than did the epidemics of ancient times; for triviality is everywhere, bringing degradation and death to souls. Before laying down the law as to man's needs and the remedies

Ordinary man is no doubt capable of providing for his needs and avoiding certain calamities, but the saint alone burns away the very roots of evil, doubtless not throughout the world, "for it must needs be that offences come", but in particular surroundings and according to the economy of Providence.

It would certainly be absurd to assert that human beings are fundamentally bad; but with the best will in the world one cannot find in man the innocence of virgin nature. As Moses intoned, man is "like grass which groweth up . . . in the evening it is cut down, and withereth", which would be in no way abnormal if man were merely grass; but we are beings much too conscious, precisely, to be "fully entitled" to be as wretched as in fact we are. If man is good, why seek to protect him against himself—for what enemy has he outside his own species—and if religion is a human thing, since there is no God, how is it reasonable to reproach it with ruined man? And if human evil has a source outside man, whence does it come? Not from animality, for an animal, however savage, is incapable of human perversion.

What anti-traditional humanitarianism has completely lost sight of is that evils on earth are inevitable because the world is not God or because the effect is not the Cause; the discrepancy between the two terms must therefore be manifested in the term that is relative, and this is precisely the meaning of suffering and death. Man escapes this fatality only in the Absolute; we do not say that he cannot avoid certain evils on a limited plane, but we do say that he cannot avoid evil as such, which is an entirely different thing. The attitude of convinced optimists is, for all intents and purposes, to choose the world while wishing it were not the world. "Seek ye first the kingdom of God, and His righteousness; and all these things shall be added unto you," says the Gospel.

This digression allows us to assess more easily the danger that modern influences involve for non-doctrinal and "practical" *bhakti*; one can see among certain Hindu reformers how a profane humanitarianism, which they evidently did not suppose to be such, nevertheless redounded upon their "theology": in order to save God's honor or excuse His existence, it was necessary to reduce God to the col-

---

they require, it is necessary to know what man is; it is necessary to envisage the human being in his totality or not be concerned with him at all.

lective soul, even if this meant leaving Him a place in an ill-defined subjective experience. In a general way, one thing Orientals who seek to be spiritual as well as westernized seem not to understand is that if their fathers had thought "freely" like themselves as little as two centuries ago, there would today be no spirituality, either "conservative" or still less "progressive"; in other words these people live on a heritage they despise and are squandering unwittingly, just as Westerners have already been doing for a long time. Modernist influence is everywhere destroying the doctrinal foundations and introducing all kinds of errors and prejudices; the result is a great deal of confusion and above all a curious lack of any sense of proportion.[13] Let us note in this same line of thought the extreme liberty that is taken with the

---

[13] It frequently happens that anglicized Hindus, like other Asians, mention in the same breath names like Jesus and Gandhi, Shankara and Kierkegaard, Buddha and Goethe, the Holy Virgin and Mrs. X., or affirm that such and such a German musician was a *yogin* or that the French Revolution was a mystical movement, and so on and so forth. This fact, we must say, reveals a total ignorance of certain differences of level that are nonetheless of capital importance—we would readily say differences of "reality"—as well as a strange lack of sensibility; it also shows a tendency to simplification, doubtless owing to the more or less unconscious idea that only "realization" counts and not "theory", from which arises a completely misplaced and openly feckless contempt for the objective discernment of phenomena. Is it then necessary to remind people that a "great incarnation", who conforms to cyclic laws and in whom the Deity is manifested in a "direct" and "active" way, differs totally not only from ordinary men, "geniuses" included, but even from a "lesser incarnation", which takes place in a human receptacle where the divine manifestation is in a sense "indirect" and "passive"? Hinduism nevertheless distinguishes with complete clarity between these two kinds of *Avatâra*, not to mention other subdivisions that need not concern us here; it is plain how much forgetfulness can result from a contempt of orthodoxy. Apart from this distinction, it is even more clearly necessary not to confuse the sacred and the profane nor above all the traditional and the anti-traditional: it is inexcusable to confuse a "thinker" who is a stranger to all tradition, and thus *a fortiori* profane, not only with a saint—who derives by definition from tradition and the sacred—but even with a traditional authority; "genius" is entirely independent of this question, for the least that can be said about it is that an "error of genius" has no value at all with regard to the truth. A typical example of neo-Hindu deviation is Swami Yogananda, founder in the United States of a "Self-Realization Fellowship" (SRF!), whose president (!) is—or was—an American woman. On the other hand we find the "discerning of spirits" present to an eminent degree in a man like Coomaraswamy, and we are not alone in hoping that his influence will grow in his own country: "While we in India are being swept by these ideologies from the modern West and would cry at any call to preserve tradition as *atavism*, a steadily

doctrine of the *Kali-Yuga* and the *Kalki-Avatâra*—the "dark age" and the "universal Messiah"—a doctrine whose importance is such that no Revelation can ignore it, whatever its symbolism, which is to say that it constitutes a criterion of orthodoxy and thereby of spiritual purity and wholeness. Since this truth, which is Christian as well as Hindu, being indeed found everywhere, excludes evolutionism, it is a bulwark of tradition against the most pernicious errors, so that its rejection— conscious or unconscious—opens the door to every kind of betrayal and corruption. We do not deny that evolution exists within certain limits, as is indeed evident enough, but we do deny that it is a universal principle, hence a law that affects and determines all things, including the immutable; evolution and degeneration can moreover go hand in hand, each then occurring on a different plane. Be that as it may, what has to be categorically rejected is the idea that truth evolves or that revealed doctrines are the product of an evolution.

*
⋊   ⋆

If true *jnâna* "is" orthodoxy by definition, *bhakti* for its part "has need" of orthodoxy—not perhaps in the case of a given *bhakta* taken in isolation and enjoying an infused and supraformal grace, but in itself and in relation to collective life, to traditional continuity. *Bhakti* cannot be a kind of "art for art's sake", that is, a self-sufficing experience claiming to be an end in itself; it is no doubt true that "all is love", but this does not mean that "love is all", which is to say "no matter what"; to strip love of its metaphysical substance and majesty is to risk depriving it of all truth and efficacy; in other words it is to destroy with the left hand what the right has built up. A particularly regrettable aspect of this leveling out is a direct or indirect contempt for the hierarchies willed

growing community of savants in the West has come to believe in the wisdom of the teachings of Coomaraswamy. . . . The earlier we garner up the remnants of our traditional culture, the greater the prospect of the ark of the new and free India saving itself from deluge" (Dr. V. Raghavan, in *Homage to Ananda K. Coomaraswamy*). "Let no man [in India] presume to invoke the name of Coomaraswamy . . . if [he] still, for [his] child, considers English a more important study than the *Shâstras*, or if [he] continues to value Matriculation or a B.A. above *dharma*" (Marco Pallis, in *Homage to Ananda K. Coomaraswamy*).

by God or for the symbols and institutions of God more generally, as if dogmas could be transcended from below and as if love could be made perfect without respect for traditional values to the extent they represent Revelation. It is not enough to know that dogmas have a limitative character; it is necessary to understand as well that they have a positive value, not only through their metaphysical and mystical contents, which link them with eternal truths, but also through their purely human opportuneness—social, psychological, and so forth—as foreseen by divine Wisdom and Mercy. In any case it cannot be assumed that all love is impeccable and that here below there are differences only of quantity, as if behind some enthusiasm or other there might not be lurking all the sterile and insolent casualness of the man who despises the sacred framework and replaces it with a concocted zeal of his own. If it is necessary to base oneself *a priori* on the formal elements of tradition, this is because we are not able to pass beyond the world of forms without finding some point of support on the formal plane itself; none come to the "Father" except by the "Son", as the Gospel puts it. The *sannyâsin* abandons rites, certainly, but he abandons them ritually and does not propose that anyone so choosing should abandon them just anyhow; he is without caste and is able to take no account of castes, but he does not dream of preaching their abolition.[14]

We could also express ourselves this way: the modern "spiritualism" of India, whether based upon *bhakti* or *jnâna* or both at once—to say nothing of those who think they can do better than the sages of old—is characterized not only by a too unilateral confidence in a given "means", but also and above all by the fact of neglecting with remarkable unawareness the human foundations—the "human climate", if one prefers[15]—the integrity of which is guaranteed only by tradition and the sacred. Spiritual "short cuts" certainly exist and cannot but

---

[14] In Japan, the devotees of *nembutsu* abandon other practices not because they scorn them, but because, believing themselves to be fallen and incapable, they scorn themselves. In Hesychasm, the monk or the hermit who has advanced in the "Jesus Prayer" or in the invocation of the Name of Jesus alone can be exempted from attending services, but this is clearly not equivalent to rejecting them.

[15] Some will perhaps point out that the Amidism of Honen and Shinran also neglects the "human foundations", but that would be a false deduction, for in this case the foundations are to be found within the civilization of ancient Japan,

exist since they are possible; but being founded on pure intellection on the one hand and a subtle and rigorous technique on the other, and bringing into play both the constitution of the microcosm and universal analogies, such short cuts require an intellectual preparation and a psychological conditioning anchored in the tradition, without which they remain ineffective or still worse lead in the opposite direction. This is the sin committed by the protagonists of such and such a *yoga*, who believe they must offer the least apt and least informed people a "way" that is "purely scientific" and "non-sectarian", one "discovered" by ancient sages but "freed from all superstition" and "scholasticism", that is, freed—all things considered—from every traditional safeguard and indeed from every adequate reason for existing.

Nevertheless in this order of things, though only in the sphere of *bhakti*, there are some cases where it can be asked whether such irregularities are not the work of the divine Mercy, which—in view of the chaotic and exceptional circumstances of our time—goes beyond certain boundaries in order to reach hearts in the very depths of ignorance and triviality; but we do not propose to settle every aspect of this question, leaving it for God alone to judge. What may well be asked, however, is whether certain advantages can counterbalance certain disadvantages, and in the majority of cases it is easy to recognize that this is not so; graces that manifest themselves despite everything—considering the miseries of human ignorance—could not compensate for the progressivist virus that falsifies minds and above all could not justify or sanction it.[16] We can admit that a *bhakta* of the naive and "child of God" type is a victim rather than someone accountable since the traditional environment is lacking, for he has "harmlessness" without having the "wisdom" which, precisely, ought to be found within the general environment, within the cultural framework that "thinks for him"; the simple *bhakta*, much more than the *bhakta* of

which like every integrally traditional civilization excludes the modern tendencies to triviality, belittling, and falsification; this is an essential point.

[16] The fact that darkness does not comprehend it cannot prevent the shining of the light, provided that the possibility of some good survives. It may happen that a false and "stupid" work of art conveys a heavenly grace as if by accident; Mercy violates certain conditions laid down by the very nobility of grace, and this in response to the fervor and sincerity of some particular soul and because of the irremovable nature of the environment in question.

intellectual type, has the right to be a child, but he is nonetheless running the risks that may result from this condition, and more important he makes others run them; it is always painful, and often worrisome, to see children taking themselves for adults.

We have just criticized inordinate confidence in "means" alone; on the Christian side there is a tendency toward the opposite mistake of hastening to declare on every occasion that "prescriptions" are ineffective, that everything depends on charity and grace; it is perfectly legitimate and sufficient, however, to describe such and such a revealed "technique" as being endowed with salvific power for the simple reason that putting such a technique into practice under normal conditions will entail without further question the purifications and virtues necessary for perfection, or else it will be abandoned because of its difficulty, a difficulty not of principle but of fact; to add that all depends upon grace is to make too much of the obvious, as if one were to say that the possibility of crossing a street depends on predestination.[17] The simple and direct expressions of Hinduism are elliptical, but not simplistic; what we criticize in so many modern Hindus is their forgetfulness of the indispensable "human climate" such as exists in every society having a sacred character, and not the innate tendency of Hindus to avoid being hampered by superfluous verbal precautions. In our day Asians too readily generalize certain "categories" and "implications" inherent in their respective civilizations and attribute to man as such various qualifications resulting from their own traditional environment, whether the causes of these qualities are near at hand or remote; there is here an "optical illusion" resulting above all from a lack of experience and of terms of comparison and from a failure to stand back from oneself. Asians have difficulty in conceiving

---

[17] In an analogous order of ideas, we have read somewhere that it is possible to love a spiritual practice as one loves a glass of wine, for example, and that this is not true mortification—a completely useless overstatement, for what counts here is precisely that prayer is not a glass of wine; the element that distinguishes it is the divine action of which it is the vehicle and whose savor we are able to love more than anything else, which is by no means such a bad thing at least in men of sound mind, who are the only ones who count in this respect. We are the last to deny that it may be necessary ultimately to transcend this kind of attachment like all the others; indeed we go much further and say that it is necessary, in principle and on condition of possessing the corresponding sapiential vocation, to transcend attachment to every "mythology" and to renounce all such "consolation".

to what extent modern Westerners differ from them, just as they take little account in general of all that is implied psychologically by the objects and activities characterizing the world of the machine and the demagogue; a candid and impeccable logic is quite ineffectual in this order of things.[18]

*

*   *

In order to understand certain errors of neo-bhaktism or neo-Hinduism in general,[19] it is necessary to remember that the opposition "orthodoxy-heterodoxy" unfortunately does not always coincide—in fact far from it—with the opposition "piety-worldliness"; this paradox is a favorite haunt of Satan, for there is here a fruitful ground for all

[18] Paradoxically enough, this lack of discernment or this need to glorify what one cannot avoid is to be found in all religious circles and is explained by a mentality grown largely profane and also by a certain "inferiority complex". One would think that many believers from all kinds of backgrounds had never heard of the prophecies concerning the end of the world and the reign of Antichrist, or that they cannot read. To the reproach of "having pretensions to divine wisdom while excelling in knowledge of things of this world" (Guillaume de Saint-Amour), Saint Thomas Aquinas replies quite justly: "They doubtless hold a false opinion who pretend that it is a matter of indifference regarding the truth of faith whether one has any particular thought on the subject of creation, provided one has a right opinion about God: for an error concerning the creation engenders a false science of God." It is here a question of the immediate qualitative knowledge of phenomena and not their scientific analysis: what matters is not to know that the earth turns round the sun or to grasp the molecular structure of matter, but to discern the cosmic value—oriented toward the absolute Cause—of the phenomena that surround us and according to the way they surround us. Be that as it may, what we wish to refute is the "angelism" of those who judge it to be immaterial whether one believes in evolution, progress, science, and the machine, provided one blesses oneself; now to believe in evolution with all this implies is obviously to have a false opinion "on the subject of creation"; the aberrations of a Teilhard de Chardin show clearly how such opinions implicitly ruin "sacred science", for they cut it off from the light in advance.

[19] It must be emphasized that in all these considerations it is not a question of the strictly traditional spirituality of India, always supposing this remains wholly intact, nor exclusively of specifically modernist movements, which as such have no interest for us, but of the contamination of the Hindu spirit by modern ideas and tendencies and hence of a state of affairs that is fluid and hard to define.

sorts of seductions and hypocrisies; it is in short to speculate deceitfully on the difference of planes separating doctrinal truth from virtue. Nothing is more agreeable to the Evil One than the cries of indignation of the heretic against the occasional vice of the orthodox or the pharisaical condemnation by some orthodox person, or by a given level of orthodoxy, of a spiritual value that is misunderstood; the genesis of the modern West and the easy and rapid modernization of the East are to be explained in large part by these inseparable oscillations. The rhythm of universal decadence, which some call "History", proceeds by reactions; it includes a first movement: the transforming of legitimate things into caricatures; then a second movement: reacting against these caricatures from below by abolishing their positive content, that is, replacing by errors the truths they disfigure. Or again: heretics of every kind attribute an absolute significance to partial truths, which is the very definition of error; but in our day error is absolved because a partial truth is necessarily found within it, and so it goes. In the same line of thought, but from a somewhat different point of view, we would like to draw attention to the following: when one feels astonishment at the foundering of the oriental civilizations, one forgets that the immense majority of men are "worldly" and not "spiritual" and that modern civilization—the only "worldly" civilization among all the others—must exercise a veritable fascination over worldly men still living under a theocracy; the converse holds true for Westerners endowed with an exceptional contemplativity who discover Asia and by this roundabout means perhaps rediscover Christianity with all it contains that is "Asian" and timeless. The decline of oriental civilizations is also explained by the fact that tradition presents—accidentally and through human weakness—an aspect of constraint, narrowness, routine, even unintelligence, so that modernism readily appears to the "worldly" under the fallacious guise of freedom, universality, greatness, not to mention "sincerity", which is all too often merely a form of cynicism devoid of all charity; but there is here an immense illusion—such as would prefer a healthy dog to a leprous saint—as well as a blindness that renders one incapable of distinguishing triviality from nobility. The evils of the old civilizations are inevitable as collective facts, but escape from them must be "from above" and not "from below".[20]

---

[20] There are neo-Hindu "reformers" who want to "reject all these fables about cults, this blowing of conches, this ringing of bells" and even "all pride of knowl-

To sum up we would formulate our thoughts as follows: if truth is a good—and even the most precious good for a being endowed with intelligence—charity cannot dispense with it. True charity will seek as far as possible to give only unmixed good and to offer every man the nourishment that suits him best, whether "dogmatic" or "dualistic", as some would say;[21] this charity is always conscious of its responsibilities and does not launch out into a short-sighted and double-edged idealism; it never forgets the weakness of human nature nor the needs—as well as the dangers—which result from it and which every traditional wisdom has foreseen far better than the most generous dreams of men could ever do.

edge and study of the *Shâstras* and all those methods for attaining personal deliverance". But if the Brahmans had not blown conches during thousands of years, none of you "reformers" of India would even exist!

[21] Those who consider the fact of seeing evil to be a proof of wickedness ("the good see nothing but good everywhere", and so forth) are the first to see evil once it is a question of orthodoxy, dogmas, cults, priestly institutions; in practice it is evil itself that profits most from their "universal Love".

The Doctrine of Illusion

It may seem strange that it should be necessary to underscore the fact that the metaphysical doctrine of illusion is not just a solution of convenience and does not justify reducing everything on the plane of phenomena to a single level. Certainly, reality is reality, and illusion is illusion; but no "realization" permits us to believe that two and two make five or that black is white on the pretext that numbers and colors are illusory. Even so there is a weakness here, which we encounter within the shadow of an "operative" *jnâna* and which tends against the nature of things to reduce everything to a single intellectual and experimental motif and thus to blur all qualitative differences, whereas in reality the function of the Intellect is the reverse, which is to say that it discriminates "outwardly" to the extent it unifies "inwardly"; metaphysical synthesis is not a physical leveling.[1] This supposedly Vedantic leveling becomes particularly troublesome when it attacks sacred things that it judges inferior: when, for example, it loses sight of the fact that religion—which it labels "sectarianism"—is not of human origin and that there are things which, though on a level below that of supreme knowledge, are nonetheless the will of God and not inventions of man; the miracles of Christ are not "occult powers" (*siddhi*s) that can be exercised or not, but divine manifestations, hence facts that elude all psychological evaluation, and Christ is not a man who became wise, but Wisdom become man.[2] That all is *Âtmâ*—or *Mâyâ*, according to the point of view—certainly does not authorize us

---

[1] If "clay and gold are one", as Ramakrishna declared after a mystical experience, basing himself moreover on the Scriptures, it is obvious that this statement is valid in the spiritual sense, but not on the physical plane; there is in fact no difference between precious and common materials when regarded from the subjective point of view of detachment or from the objective point of view of existential limits; but this transcending of differences cannot be realized if one starts by repudiating differences on their own plane, for the sublime is not to be sought in the absurd.

[2] No doubt it is necessary to set aside such judgments as are to be explained either by a "traditionally legitimate" ignorance or by a revealed perspective that provides grounds for a particular interpretation of certain facts-symbols; this second possibility in any case concerns Semites rather than Hindus.

to "take a rope for a snake", as the Vedantists say, quite the contrary; there is no true synthesis without discernment. What is *Vedânta* if not a "discrimination" (*viveka*) between the real and the unreal and an "investigation" (*vichâra*) into our true nature? Now discrimination in the "vertical sense" (between *Sachchidânanda* and *nâma-rûpa*) does not go without an equivalent discrimination in the "horizontal sense" with regard to the "qualities" (*gunas*).

Certain theorists of the *Vedânta*, anxious to buttress their conviction about the exclusive reality of the Self, the "inward Witness" of all thought, feel obliged to deny the reality of the object as if it were the "mental" that creates the objective world—the Scriptures teach the contrary[3]—and as if one term of a polarity had any meaning without the opposite and complementary term. In thus reducing the object to the subject, no explanation is given either of the cause of the world or of its homogeneity, which makes all men see the same sun and not something else. The only valid argument is forgotten, namely, that the world is not the illusion of the particular individual—otherwise each individual would dream a different world—but of a collectivity or plurality of collectivities, which are superimposed on or interpenetrate one another; this "collective subject" embraces all humanity and, on a vaster scale, all terrestrial creatures. The empirical homogeneity of the world is then explained by solidarity within a cosmic dream, which is marked by a common "sensibility"; a mountain is a mountain and not a dream even for an ant, or ants would be going through rocks and climbing in the void. There is thus a multiform "earthly being", which is a state of existence having innumerable degrees or "compartments" and the center of which is the human state: all the subjects contained in this collective subject will have homogeneous reactions in the sense that for all of them the sun gives heat, light, and life or that for all a rock is impenetrable, and so forth. This "being" must moreover extend beyond terrestrial limits, for it is more than probable that this something that causes us the sensation "sun" causes the same sensation in extraterrestrial beings, so that the problem of objectivity—or the collective dream—scarcely stops at the limits of any given subjec-

---

[3] "Thus appearances (external objects) are not caused by mind, nor is mind the product of appearances" (*Mândûkya-Kârikâ* of Gaudapada, 4, 54). Shankara-charya takes up this thesis in his commentary.

tive universe; a particular cosmos is a closed system only in a relative sense, for Existence is one. It is in fact only the total Universe that we can qualify as a "dream" pure and simple since an ordinary dream presupposes by definition a perfect subjectivity, and this condition, which implies that vision should be shared by no other subject—unless by subjective coincidence—is fulfilled only in the "dream" of the universal Soul, where the subject is unique; in this case the word "dream" is only another term for "illusion" or *mâyâ*.[4] The star-filled sky is not a dream insofar as we see it or all men see it, but insofar as the universal Soul "conceives" it in a play that is eternally free, having no other motive than Beatitude; the starry vault is not an "imagination" of our individual consciousness but of a "universal layer" of our consciousness, hence of a consciousness that immensely surpasses the ego, whence the homogeneity of the empirical world. It is "universal Man" who dreams,[5] and we dream in him and with him.

In other terms: for the Absolute, there is no difference between objects perceived in the waking state or in the dream state; but from the point of view of relative reality—which we cannot hold to be nonexistent since we find ourselves in it and act on that basis—there is between these two states an eminent difference in the sense that the first has more universality, hence more reality, than the second. The proof: first, external objects are perceived by several subjects and even by innumerable subjects in space and time, according to circumstances, whereas in a dream there is only a single subject, who in reality is also the object since he creates the images out of his own substance; second, external objects can themselves be subjects, and in this case it is evident *a priori* that the fact of being perceived by anyone at all neither adds nor subtracts any reality; third, those who profess an absolute indistinction between the states of waking and dream know when they are awake that the world is illusory, which they cannot know when they are dreaming, and this proves that for the subject as well the waking state takes precedence in its degree of universality over the beclouding of dreams; fourth, those who profess an absolute

---

[4] Let us note that *mâyâ* possesses not only the aspect of "illusion", but also that of "universal unfolding", "divine art", "cosmic magic"; but in the end the meaning of illusion is incontestable, since to believe in the absolute reality of the ego and the world is, according to the Vedantists, an effect of "ignorance".

[5] Or *Virâj*, the divine Intelligence insofar as it "conceives" the physical world.

indistinction between the two states behave as if they did not believe in it, since they eat, talk, and run if they must when chased by a bull. Objection will no doubt be made that the sage has no need to concern himself with relative reality and therefore with degrees of universality; we reply: yes he must, since he is concerned with it in any case, which deprives him of any right to claim to consider the Absolute exclusively; whoever has eyes and ears is obliged to discern relativities, with or without a spiritual vision of *Âtmâ*. If a man dreams of eating, he has the excuse of not acting freely or with full lucidity;[6] but if he eats when awake while denying in an unconditional manner the qualitative ontological difference between the two states, he has no excuse, since he believes he is dreaming and knows the dream is illusory; actions whose sole excuse in a dream is that they are involuntary do not need to be performed voluntarily. Moreover, in dreaming it happens to all of us that we are able to accomplish all sorts of desirable miracles: jumping over precipices, floating lightly in empty space like a bird, and so on; let him who believes that everything is a dream and subjectivity do half as much in the waking state if he is sincere! If the opinion that confuses the states of waking and dreaming unconditionally were well founded and if these two states were equivalent on the plane itself of relativity—whereas in reality they are so only under the gaze of the Absolute—it would make no difference whether a man was a sage dreaming he was a fool or a fool dreaming he was a sage.

The great question to be asked here is: who is the subject?[7] The fact that we can in no way cause a mountain to stop existing—as we

---

[6] A prayer or an invocation made in a dream has merit, however, whereas a sin committed in a dream does not count, which shows that Mercy does not admit of symmetry between good and evil and also that dreaming has an aspect of reality, just as the waking state has an aspect of dream or illusion.

[7] The *de facto* ambiguity of this question is in part explained by the fact that Hindus, who knew what was implied in such matters, have never made a point in their expositions, which are deliberately elliptical and centered on the essential, of offering precisions that seem to them pointless; but one must not take dialectical syntheses for mere simplifications and draw absurd conclusions from the doctrine of illusion, an error of which the ancient Vedantists were clearly not guilty, or they would have been common solipsists. Schopenhauer was wrong in thinking that solipsism is logically irrefutable, but right in declaring solipsists ripe for the lunatic asylum.

can sometimes do in a dream—proves that our particular "I", while being for the mountain an accidental subject, is nonetheless not the creator subject on which the mountain, insofar as it is an illusion, depends and that the mountain, though completely illusory on the plane of the universal subject and from the point of view of our Intellect, nonetheless possesses a relative reality for our ego and even has more reality than our imaginations. Once again, it is not possible in sound logic for a man to deny that Reality, as well as being absolute, comprises degrees and at the same time to accept the fact that he exists and that in consequence he acts; one cannot at the same time both exist and deny Existence or act and deny the cause of activity.

Now if we cannot suppose that the world is only a product— caused by what?—of our minds, no more can we suppose that the evil we discern in the world is only an objectification—in what?—of our own defects and that for the good man everything is good; if it is all to end with an abdication of intelligence, coupled with a facile and inoperative monism, it is certainly useless to resort to a "way of knowledge". It is true that "evil", or what we refer to as such, is reduced in the final analysis to a tendency that cannot not be and that is part of the universal equilibrium; but on the plane of cosmic coagulations— whether it is a question of the "external" world or the soul—this does not prevent there being phenomena that are either in keeping with or opposed to pure Being (*Sat*, whence *sattva*), nor does it mean that creatures endowed with understanding should fail to recognize them; to affirm the contrary is to disavow all the sacred Scriptures, to say nothing of simple common sense. In metaphysics, as in every other realm, it is necessary to know how to put everything in its place.

As for the question of the "origin" of illusion, it is among those questions that can be resolved—or rather there is nothing in it to resolve—though this resolution cannot be adjusted to suit all logical needs; there are demonstrations which, whether they are understood or not, are sufficient in themselves and indeed constitute pillars of metaphysical doctrine. Let us limit ourselves here to recalling what we have already said elsewhere,[8] namely, that the infinitude of Reality

---

[8] In *Perspectives spirituelles et faits humains*. We believe that a certain repetition in our writings can only add to their clarity, given the importance or the difficulty of the subjects treated; repetition is moreover inevitable in matters of this kind.

implies the possibility of its own negation and that since this negation is not possible within the Absolute itself, it is necessary that this "possibility of the impossible" should be realized in an "inward dimension" that is "neither real nor unreal", a dimension that is real on its own level while being unreal in respect of the Essence; thus we are everywhere in touch with the Absolute, from which we cannot emerge but which at the same time is infinitely distant, no thought ever circumscribing it.

II

GNOSIS

Gnosis: Language of the Self

There are various ways of expressing or defining the difference between *gnosis* and love—or between *jnâna* and *bhakti*—but here we wish to consider only one criterion, and it is this: for the "volitive" or "affective" man (the *bhakta*) God is "He" and the ego is "I", whereas for the "gnostic" or "intellective" man (the *jnânin*)[1] God is "I"—or "Self"—and the ego is "he" or "the other".[2] And one sees immediately why it is the first and not the second perspective that determines all religious dogmatism: it is because the majority of men start out with certitude about the ego and not the Absolute; most are individualists and are therefore but little suited to make a "concrete abstraction" of their empirical "I", which is an intellectual and not a moral problem: in other words few have the gift of impersonal contemplativity—for it is of this we are speaking—that allows us to "let God think" within us.

The nature of pure intellection will be better understood if one takes account of this fact: the Intellect, which is One, appears in three fundamental aspects—at least to the extent we are situated in "separative illusion", which is the case for every creature as such: first, the divine Intellect, which is Light and pure Act; second, the cosmic Intellect, which is receptacle or mirror in relation to God and light in relation to man; and third, the human Intellect, which is mirror in relation

---

[1] We would as readily have said the "theosophist", but this word might give rise to confusions. That the terms "gnostic" and "theosophist" should have fallen into discredit is a bad sign, not certainly for men like Clement of Alexandria or Boehme who used them, but for the world that has occasioned and sanctioned this discredit. The same applies to the word "intellectual", whose meaning has become quite trivial. As for the term "pneumatic", it seems to us that this applies to realization alone, not to theory.

[2] It is true that most of the sapiential doctrines, taking account of the ego as a fact and conforming themselves to the "letter" of the Revelation from which they are derived, refer to the Absolute as "He", as do the "dualists" of love, but this is hardly more than a question of dialectic, which in no way modifies the fundamental perspective, as we have explained elsewhere (*Perspectives spirituelles et faits humains*, Part 4, "The *Vedânta*"). Furthermore, *Advaita Vedânta*, which is the most direct possible expression of *gnosis*, does not exclude "objectivist" formulations of the Principle, such as *Brahmâ*, *Shiva*, and other Names.

to both of the foregoing and light in relation to the individual soul;[3] one must therefore be careful to distinguish within the Intellect—the divine Intellect excepted—an "uncreated" aspect, which is essential, and a "created" aspect, which is "accidental" or rather "contingent".[4] This synthetic view of things "results", one might say,[5] from the principle of non-alterity: that which is not "other" in any respect is "identical" under the relationship here being considered, so much so that intelligence as such—whether that of a man conforming to the truth or that of a plant causing it irresistibly to turn toward the light—"is" the intelligence of God; intelligence is "human" or "vegetal" only in relation to its specific limitations, and similar considerations apply to every positive quality, hence to all the virtues, which are always those of God, not of course in their diminishing accidentality, but in their content or essence.

These considerations allow us to see that the great Gospel virtues—charity, humility, poverty, childlikeness—have their final end in the "Self":[6] they represent so many negations of that ontological tumescence which is the ego, negations that are not individualistic and thereby contradictory,[7] but intellective, that is, taking their point

---

[3] Gospel sayings such as "I am the light of the world" or "No man cometh unto the Father, but by me" are applicable in all these three senses.

[4] The mystery of the "universal Spirit" (*Al-Rûh*) in Islam is that one is not able to say of it either that it is "created" or that it is "uncreated"; the same mystery is found in the Intellect that we have called "human" and that Meister Eckhart defined in an ambiguous manner.

[5] The frequent use of quotation marks results from the fact that expressions that are simply logical do not always keep step—indeed this is far from the case—with spiritual reality. It is also true that the meanings of many words have contracted with usage or that they have given way to associations of ideas that are more or less restrictive, to say nothing of the fact that the modern reader reads less easily "between the lines" than did the ancient reader, and this requires more precisions and shades of meaning.

[6] We could say as much about the commandments of the Decalogue: in the final analysis each indicates an aspect of the Self, and each transgression reveals an aspect of the ego as such. The "chosen People" is the soul that is "naturally" idolatrous and rebellious, but "supernaturally" redeemed by the Messiah, who is Grace or Intellect.

[7] A guilt complex and a compulsion of humility are the commonest expressions of this contradiction. An attitude is false to the extent it runs counter to truth;

of departure within the Self as such in conformity with the profound nature of things. In a similar way, if a sage cannot be satisfied in a definitive way with any created bliss—"the (created) Paradise is a prison for the Sufi"—this is not because of any pretension or ingratitude, far from it, but because the Intellect tends toward its Source or because the Self in us "wishes to be delivered". If Christ "is God", this is because the Intellect—"come down from Heaven"—"is the Self"; and in this sense every religion is "Christian": on the one hand each postulates the uncreated Intellect—or the *Logos*, the "uncreated Word" of God, which amounts to the same thing in regard to the "radiance" of the Intellect—and on the other hand it postulates the earthly manifestation of this Word and the deliverance brought about through it; every complete tradition postulates in the final analysis the "extinction" of the ego for the sake of the divine "I", an extinction for which the sacred Law provides an elementary framework, though the Law must remain "dualistic" in its common letter owing to the needs of the majority and consequently for reasons of social psychology. "Inwardly" every religion is the doctrine of the unique Self and its earthly manifestation, as well as the way leading to the abolition of the false self or the way of the mysterious reintegration of our "personality" in the celestial Prototype; "outwardly" the religions are "mythologies" or, more precisely, symbolisms designed for different human receptacles and displaying by their limitations, not a contradiction *in divinis*, but on the contrary a mercy. A doctrine or way is exoteric insofar as it is obliged to take account of individualism—the fruit not so much of passion itself as of the influence of passion on thought—and to veil the equation Intellect-Self under a mythological or moral "imagery", whether there is an element of historicity or not; and a doctrine is esoteric insofar as it communicates the very essence of our universal position, our situation between nothingness and Infinity. Esoterism looks to the nature of things and not merely to our human eschatology; it does not view the Universe starting from man, but "starting from God".[8]

true humility, the kind that is most efficacious, is an impersonal "non-pride", which remains independent of the alternative "humiliation-flattery" and avoids all unhealthy preoccupation with the "I". The fundamental virtues are centered in God, not in man.

[8] "It is for certain chosen men, who have been allowed to pass from faith to *gnosis*, that the sacred mysteries of wisdom have been preserved under the veil of par-

The exoteric mentality, with its unilateral logic and a "rationalism" that is somewhat "passional", scarcely conceives that there are questions to which the answer is at once "yes" and "no"; it is always afraid of falling into "dualism", "pantheism", "quietism", or something of the kind. In metaphysics as in psychology it is sometimes necessary to resort to ambiguous answers; for example, to the question: the world, "is it" God? we reply: "no", if by the "world" is understood ontological manifestation as such, that is, in its connection with existential or demiurgic separativity; "yes", if by the "world" is understood manifestation insofar as it is causally or substantially divine, there being nothing outside of God; in the first case God is exclusive and transcendent Principle, and in the second, total Reality or universal and inclusive Substance. God alone "is"; the world is a limited "divine aspect", for it cannot—on pain of absurdity—be a nothingness on its own level. To affirm on the one hand that the world has no "divine quality" and on the other that it is real apart from God and that it never ceases to be so amounts to admitting two Divinities, two Realities, two Absolutes.

What is "incarnation" for Christianity is "revelation" or "descent" for the other two monotheistic religions. The truth that only divine manifestation "is the Self", to the exclusion of every human counterfeit, becomes exoterically: only a particular divine manifestation—to the exclusion of all others—is the Self. It could also be said on the level of the microcosm that the Intellect alone, and no other human faculty, is the Self—not reason nor imagination nor memory nor feeling nor the faculties of sensory perception—even though, in connection with existential structures, everything reflects or "is" the Self in some way or another. This exclusive value of "incarnation", besides its spiritual significance, clearly possesses a historically literal meaning as well, which is legitimate when one considers the particular human cosmos where this divine manifestation has taken place, this being in the case of Christ the world of the Roman Empire and in a larger sense

---

ables" (Clement of Alexandria, *Stromateis*, 6, 126). This does not mean that the parables do not contain a meaning intended for all Christians, though having to be hidden provisionally from unbelievers, but that they convey at the same time a meaning that is specifically gnostic or metaphysical, hence incomprehensible to the majority of Christians themselves. Christ's command not to cast pearls before swine nor to give that which is holy to dogs cannot have a meaning that is merely temporally limited and reduced to a question of outward expedience.

the world of those whom the particular grace of Christ "has chosen", whatever their country of origin; but the literalist interpretation becomes unacceptable whenever an attempt is made to add some fact or other, even a sacred fact, to metaphysical truth, as if the latter were incomplete without it—whereas all possible facts are already included in this truth—and as if metaphysical truth were subject to time. Let us take another example: the Koranic affirmation that "God alone is God" means that there is no Self but the Self, but exoterically it implies that God could not manifest Himself as such "outside Himself", which amounts to denying the phenomenon of "incarnation"; but in every case of this kind esoterism "restores" the total truth on the plane of principles. All things considered the difference between Christian and Muslim *gnosis* is essentially this: whereas Christian *gnosis* projects the mystery of the God-Man, and thereby the mystery of the Trinity, into the soul of the gnostic, as is shown for example by certain Eckhartian texts, Sufism for its part sees "unification" (*tawhîd*) or the "unity of Existence"—or rather of "universal Reality", *wahdat al-Wujûd*, sometimes translated as the "Supreme Identity"—as rising from the very nature of the divine Unity.[9]

The exoteric distinction between "true religion" and "false religions" is replaced for the gnostic by the distinction between *gnosis* and beliefs or between essence and forms.[10] The sapiential perspective alone is an esoterism in the absolute sense; in other words it alone is necessarily and integrally esoteric because it alone reaches beyond all relativities.

---

[9] According to *gnosis*, the Islamic formula *Lâ ilâha illâ 'Llâh* means that "there is no 'me' except it be I"—hence no real or positive ego except the Self—a meaning that springs again from expressions such as the *Anâ 'l-Haqq* ("I am the Truth") of al-Hallaj or the *Subhânî* ("Glory to Me") of Bayazid. The Prophet himself expressed the same mystery in these terms: "He who has seen me has seen the Truth (God)"—that is, God cannot be seen except through His receptacle or, in a more general but less direct sense, through His symbol—and also: "I am He and He is I, save that I am who I am and He is who He is"; "I have been charged with fulfilling my mission since the best of the ages of Adam (the origin of the world), from one age to another until this age where I am."

[10] If *gnosis* is the doctrine of the Self in relation to the pole "subject", it will be the doctrine of the Essence in relation to the pole "object": "The knowledge that recognizes in all beings one unique, imperishable, indivisible essence, although scattered among separate objects, knows that this knowledge proceeds from *sattva* (the 'luminous' or 'ascending' tendency)" (*Bhagavad Gîtâ*, 18:20).

*

*   *

God is "Light" "before" He is "Heat", if it may be so expressed; *gnosis* "precedes" love, or rather love "follows" *gnosis*, for *gnosis* encompasses love after its own fashion, whereas love is nothing other than the beatitude "emerging" from *gnosis*. One can love the false without love ceasing to be what it is; but one cannot "know" the false in the same way, which is to say that knowledge cannot be deluded about its object without ceasing to be what it is; error always implies a privation of knowledge, whereas sin does not imply a privation of will. Therein lies a most important application of the symbolism of the Adamic "androgyne" and the creation of Eve: it is only after the "coming forth" of love outside knowledge—whence the polarization "intelligence-will"—that the temptation and the fall could, or can, take place; in one sense the rational faculty became detached from the Intellect through the intervention of the will, having been seduced by the "serpent" and become "free" from below, that is, able to choose between true and false; the choice of the false having become possible, it was bound to appear with the force of a torrential seduction; reason, mother of the "wisdom according to the flesh", is the "natural" child issued from Adam's sin. Here the serpent is what Hindus understand by *tamas*: the "descending", "darkening", "compressive", and at the same time "dissipating" and "dissolving" tendency, which on contact with the human person becomes personified as Satan. All things considered, the question: "Why does evil exist?" amounts to asking why there is an existence; the serpent is to be found in Paradise because Paradise exists. Paradise without the serpent would be God.

Man complains of his sufferings, such as separation and death; but has he not inflicted them *a priori* upon the Self by his very egoity? Is not individuation a separation from the divine "I", and is not the ego a death from the point of view of infinite Life? It will be objected that we are not responsible for our existence; but man in his actions ceaselessly recreates the responsibility that he thinks he does not have; in this, taken together with what has been considered already, lies the deeper meaning of original sin.[11] Man suffers because he wants to be "self"

---

[11] There are apparent heresies which are not false in themselves, but which refer to an "ontological stratum" deeper than that of ordinary theological concepts:

in opposition to the "Self", and Christ effaces this fundamental "sin" by assuming the suffering that is its result. He is the Self holding out a hand to the "me"; man must "lose his life", the life of the ego, in order to keep it, the life of the Self. In his solar aspect—which implies the warmth of love as well as the light of wisdom—Christ is the Self that unites and absorbs all beings. The Self became ego that the ego might become Self; the divine "Subject" became cosmic "object" because the "object" must once again become the "Subject".[12] The Self alone is "itself"; the ego is "other", from which comes its initial imbalance and insatiability: all it does is search for itself; in whatever it does it is in pursuit of that transcendent and absolute "I" in which the beatitudes are inward and permanent instead of being scattered about a world that is endlessly deceitful. "The Kingdom of God is within you."

If "that which is born of the Spirit is Spirit", this is because the Spirit is the Self and because there is no other knowing or loving Subject in the infinite Bliss; similarly, if he that is "born of the Spirit"[13] is like

---

the refusal to attribute an absolute scope to "original sin" proceeds, when it has an adequate motive, from a more fundamental and more "neutral" vision of our human reality, one which however is less accessible to a given mentality and therefore also less opportune for a given morality; in the same way "quietism", insofar as it contains a legitimate element, stands nearer to contemplation and *gnosis* than does the accumulating of merits: "There is no lustral water like unto knowledge," says the Law of Manu. One can regret, without being unrealistic, that western theology has not known a gradation of truths according to their level of validity: having chosen but one level, or more or less so—namely, what was appropriate for the collectivity—this theology first impoverished itself and then indirectly provoked "ruptures", which have ended by threatening its very existence.

[12] "And the light shineth in darkness; and the darkness comprehended it not": the ego has not understood that its immortal reality—or the Intellect—is none other than the Self. "Inasmuch as ye have done it unto one of the least of these my brethren, ye have done it unto Me": this is the enunciation—as Coomaraswamy so justly remarked—of the cosmic reverberation of the Self, who is the "only transmigrant" according to Shankara.

[13] "Except a man be born of water and of the Spirit, he cannot enter into the kingdom of God. That which is born of the flesh is flesh; and that which is born of the Spirit is spirit" (John 3:5-6). "Water is looked on by many traditions as the original medium of beings, and the reason lies in its symbolism . . . by which water represents *Mûla-Prakriti*; in a higher sense and by transposition, water is Universal Possibility itself; he that is 'born of water' becomes a 'son of the Virgin',

the wind, of which one "canst not tell whence it cometh, and whither it goeth", this is because, being identified with the Self, he is without origin;[14] he has come forth from the chain of cosmic causations and dwells in the Changeless. Similarly again, one can see a reference to the Self—other meanings notwithstanding—in these words: "No man hath ascended up to heaven, but he that came down from heaven." To "ascend up to heaven" is to "become Oneself", that is, to become what one had never really ceased to be inasmuch as the essence of the ego is the Self, the "Life" we obtain only by losing the life of the "me".[15]

For Plato-Socrates, the "true philosopher" is he who has consecrated himself to the "study of the separation between the soul and the body or of the liberation of the soul" and who is "always occupied with the practice of dying"; it is he who withdraws from the bodily—hence from everything in the ego that is the shadow or echo of the surrounding world—in order to be no more than absolutely pure soul, immortal Soul, Self: "The Soul-in-itself must contemplate Things-in-themselves" (*Phaedo*). Thus the criterion of truth—and the basis of conviction, this reverberation of Light in the "outward man"—is the Truth as such, the pre-phenomenal Intelligence by which "all things were made" and without which "was not anything made that was made".

---

hence an adopted brother of Christ and coinheritor of the 'Kingdom of God'. On the other hand, if one observes the fact that 'spirit' . . . is the Hebrew *Ruah* (here associated with water as a complementary principle, as at the beginning of Genesis) and that *Ruah* at the same time denotes the air, one will recognize in this the idea of purification by the elements" (René Guénon, *L'Homme et son devenir selon le Vêdânta*, Chapter 20, note).

[14] "Whence come these Buddhas? Whither vanishes this body of mine? Reflecting thus he sees that all the *Tathâgata*s come from nowhere and go nowhere" (*Pratyutpanna-Samâdhi Sûtra*, quoted by Suzuki in *Essais sur le Bouddhisme Zen*, 10: "Le Kô-an et le nemboutsu").

[15] "With Christ I must be buried," said Saint Gregory of Nazianzus, "with Christ I must rise again, and with Christ I must inherit; I must become Son of God and God himself" (*Discourse* 7, 23). "Understand who has given you to be Son of God, heir of Christ, and—to use a bold term—God himself" (*Discourse* 14, 23). "But this (the Kingdom of Heaven) consists in my view in nothing but the possession of what is most pure and most perfect. Now the most perfect thing that exists is knowledge of God" (*Discourse* 20, 12).

*

*   *

We have said previously that in the human microcosm only the Intellect "is" the Self, to the exclusion of any specifically "mental" faculty. For just as a distinction must be made between an ordinary creature and the "Word made flesh", so also is it necessary to distinguish between rational thought, which is discursive and proceeds from the mind alone, and intellective thought, which proceeds from intuition and the pure Intellect: this second mode of thought is indeed an "exteriorization for the sake of an interiorization", whereas the first is purely and simply an expression for the sake of manifestation as such. To rational thought corresponds the infrahuman world, production of the "cosmic brain", and to intellective thought corresponds the human race, expression of the "heart"; on a smaller scale and within the very framework of humanity, it is the *Avatâra* who corresponds to the second mode of thought. The entire drama of Christ or of Revelation is thus prefigured—or "post-figured", according to the point of view—in the intellectual act, whether in the original intellection or in unitive meditation; this form of thought is like a "salvific incarnation" or a "unitive incarnation" of the Heart-Intellect. In other words, it is necessary to distinguish between terrestrial thought, induced by the environment and finding its end in the environment, and celestial thought, induced by what constitutes our eternal substance and finding its end beyond ourselves and, in the final analysis, in the Self. Reason is something like a "profane intelligence"; the profane point of view springs essentially from it. It is necessary for reason to be determined, transfigured, or regenerated either by faith or by *gnosis*, which is the quintessence of faith.

Gnosis, by the very fact that it is a "knowing" and not a "willing", is centered upon "that which is" and not upon "that which ought to be"; from this there results a way of regarding the world and life that differs greatly from the way, more "meritorious" perhaps but less "true", in which volitive men regard the vicissitudes of existence. The background of the drama of life for the *bhakta* is the "Will of God" and for the *jnânin* the nature of things; for the first the acceptance of destiny results from unconditional love, hence from "that which must be", and for the second from discernment of metaphysical necessity, hence from "that which is". The *bhakta* accepts all destiny as coming from the Beloved; he also accepts it because he makes no distinction between "I" and "others" and because, this being so, he is unable to rebel against an event simply because it is he and not some other man who undergoes it; if he accepts everything through love of God, he does so as well on that very basis through love of neighbor. The attitude of the *jnânin*, on the contrary, is an impassibility founded upon discernment between the Real and the unreal: "The world is false; *Brahma* is true"; "That art Thou" (*Brahma, Âtmâ*); "Everything is *Âtmâ*"; "I am *Brahma*". Events of life arise, as do all phenomena, from the indefinitely varying combinations of the three "cosmic qualities" (the *guna*s: *sattva, rajas*, and *tamas*); these events therefore cannot not be in such measure as the world is relatively real; but as soon as this relativity is transcended, they cease to exist, and then there is no longer a "good" or an "evil", nor any karmic concatenation; the plane of the *guna*s ("simultaneous" qualities) and *karma* (composed of "successive" qualities) is as if annihilated in the undifferentiated serenity of Being or the Self. And in the same way there is no "juridical" relationship between the astonishments, anxieties, and indignations of the soul and the unconditional serenity of the Intellect, or to be more precise: between the logic of disquiet and the transcendence of serenity; the divergence is incommensurable and yet the second term is already concealed within the first, already so to speak within reach.

In the spiritual life, to speak of "willing" is to speak of "willing what is Good"; "to will what is Good" is "to will well", that is, to "will through the Good" or "through God"; instead of "to will" one could also say "to love", and instead of the "Good" one could say the "Beautiful". On the other hand, to speak of "knowing" is to speak of "knowing what is"; to speak of "knowing what is" is to speak in the final analysis of "being what knows": the Self.

*

* *

Reference has been made to the "cosmic qualities", the *guna*s, and to *karma*, as well as to the serenity that transcends all existential conditions: this serenity—or this deliverance—lies as it were at the center of existence like a kernel of peace and light; it is like a drop of saving dew in an ocean of flames. "All the universe is ablaze," said the Buddha; what we do not realize is that the existential substance is made of fire—this substance into which we are woven while yet remaining alien bodies. For the "naive" and "unrepentant" man the world is a neutral space from which he chooses the agreeable contents while believing he has the power to avoid the disagreeable if he is clever and lucky; but the man who does not know that existence is an immense conflagration has no imperative reason for wanting to get out of it, and this is why an Arab proverb says that "the summit of wisdom is the fear of God"—that is, the fear of divine afflictions, which are the price of our state of remoteness.

The kernel of light at the center of the current of forms is essentially the "remembrance of God"—which in the final analysis demands all that we are—as these Muhammadan words declare: "All that is to be found on earth is cursed save the remembrance of God," and "There is no fault greater than that of existence." "There is none good but one, that is, God," said Christ: this implies that what comes from God, His Name, and what leads to Him, the remembrance of His Name, share in His goodness. The virtual fire from which we live withdraws from things to the extent we are centered on the mystery of remembrance: things then become transparent and transmit to us rays of their immutable and blessed archetypes. We could also say that existence is made of fire to the extent it is regarded as being outside God and thereby leads to fire; it is a burning for the perverted will and an illumination for the contemplative intelligence, and it is thus at once a threat and a "consolation", enslaving seduction and liberating vision. It is the immutable and blessed archetypes that man is seeking when he attaches himself to shadows here below; and he suffers cruelly, first when the shadows disappear and later when, at death, he perceives the archetypes, from which his love for the shadows had turned him away.[16]

In its global reality, Existence is serene and not malefic; cosmic Wrath is reabsorbed in total and virginal Equilibrium. Existence in itself is the universal Virgin, who by her purity as also by her mercy vanquishes the sin of the demiurgic Eve, the bringer forth of creatures and passions; Eve, who produces, seduces, and attaches, is "eternally" vanquished by the Virgin, who purifies, pardons, and sets free.

---

[16] Music—like dance—is the art of leading terrestrial shadows back to celestial vibrations and divine archetypes. Stylization plays a similar role in the plastic arts.

For *gnosis* the existential fire is inseparable from ignorance, hence from illusion. The fundamental cause of illusion or ignorance is not however our state of fall nor some deficiency of the existential substance, but the principle of objectification, by which the pole "being" is cut off from the pure Subject; seen from this angle the universal Virgin is "illusory" as well, and so is Being insofar as it is distinct from the supra-ontological Subject, which is the Self.[17] But Existence and Being, even if they belong to the realm of *Mâyâ*, nonetheless remain beyond the current of forms and thus beyond separation, suffering, and death.

Gnosis is our participation—a participation that is certainly possible, however precarious and conditional, since we could not be in every respect absolutely "distinct" from God without having no reality at all—our participation, we say, in the "perspective" of the divine Subject, which is itself in turn beyond the separative polarity "subject-object", though this in no way signifies that it does not carry within itself, in a manner conforming to its Essence, the cause of all cosmic polarizations; what this means is that we can indeed discern something like a polarity within it, but on condition of not seeing there any separation or opposition.

*

* *

The absolute Subject carries its immediate and connatural Object within itself, and this Object is infinite Beatitude. When Hindu doctrine describes *Âtmâ* as being made up of "Being", "Consciousness", and "Bliss" (*Sat, Chit, Ânanda,* whence the divine Name *Sachchidânanda*), this enumeration means that the Subject is "Being that knows, having Beatitude for object": "being"—or "being real"—is "Consciousness" of all its possibilities; the use of the verb "to be" here is quite provisional since the Self is situated beyond ontological Unity. Now, the world is as if included within the divine Beatitude, or

---

[17] In Eckhart, Silesius, Omar Khayyam, and others, one finds allusions to this "relativity" of Being in relation to the Self. In the doctrines of India and the Far East—Shivaite *Vedânta, Mahâyâna* Buddhism, and Taoism—this idea is fundamental.

more precisely it is included as it were within Being, which is itself so to speak the "outward" dimension of Beatitude or of the Self; we say "outward" in placing ourselves at the standpoint of the world, which is the standpoint of man, for it goes without saying that there is no kind of "outwardness" within the Infinite. And this is why one says theologically that God created the world "out of goodness": "love" and "goodness" as well as "beauty" are so many aspects of Beatitude, which is identified with All-Possibility. That the world is "contained" within the divine Beatitude or Goodness means in relation to suffering—even infernal suffering—that the being always keeps the gift of existence, positive in itself, and that all suffering necessarily is limited in its nature and duration, God alone being absolute.

The subjective principle emanating from the divine Subject crosses the Universe like a ray in order to end in the multitude of egos. The formal world is characterized by the "outward limits" of its contents, therefore by a kind of indefinite segmentation;[18] thus its "subjectivity" will be multiple, whence the innumerable diversity of souls. Man marks the limit of the "creative ray" for the terrestrial world that is his; his sufficient reason consists in being this limit, that is, in providing a stop—after the manner of an echo or a mirror—to the "ray of exteriorization" of the Self; thus the human state is an exit—and the only exit for the terrestrial world—not only from this world or the formal cosmos, but even from the immense and numberless objectification that is universal Existence; being a total microcosm, a plenary "I", it is at the same time a door open toward the Self and immortality.

Is there any immortality outside the Self? Yes and no: there is also paradisiacal immortality, but it "comes to an end"—"from above"—in the final reintegration (the *mahâpralaya* of the Hindus or the end of a "life of *Brahmâ*") of Existence in the Self; but this ending precisely is a "more" and not a "less", a "fulfillment" *in divinis* and not an "abolition".

*

* *

[18] In the non-formal or supra-formal world, which is the realm of the angelic states, all things are perceived as subsisting "in the interior" of the subject, differences among the angelic subjects being marked by their modes of perception.

In one of his hymns to Hari, Shankaracharya says: "Lord, although I and Thou make but One, I belong to Thee, but not Thou to me, just as the waves belong to the sea, but not the sea to the waves." And in another hymn (*Kâshîpanchakam*), Shankara expresses himself thus: "That which is the ceasing of mental agitation and the supreme assurance; that which is the lake Manikarnika and the pilgrimage above all others; that which is the primordial and purest Ganges, river of Knowledge: this is Benares, innate Wisdom, and it is this that I am."

The Ternary Aspect of the Human Microcosm

Human life unfolds on three planes simultaneously, or rather the ego is subject to three centers of attraction, to which it responds in different ways according to its nature or worth. We live at the same time in the body, the head, and the heart, so that we may sometimes ask ourselves where the genuine "I" is located; in fact the ego proper, the empirical "I", has its sensory seat in the brain, but it readily gravitates toward the body and tends to identify itself with it, whereas the heart is the symbolic seat of the Self, of which we may or may not be aware, but which is our true existential, intellectual, and therefore universal center. This is in a sense the old triad *anima, animus, Spiritus*, with the difference however that *anima*—the "spouse" of *animus*—is the vegetative and animal psychism rather than the body itself; but there is no sharp demarcation here since we cannot dissociate the body from its sensations, which in fact constitute our lower and decentralized ego with its downward drag and dispersive tendency.

The brain is to the body what the heart is to the brain and body taken together. The body and the brain are as it were projected into the current of forms; the heart is as if immersed in the immutability of Being. Body and brain are so to speak the heart exteriorized or "extruded"; their bipolarization is explained by the very fact of their exteriorization. The formal world being made up of dualities, the Intellect, once it has been projected by virtue of its "fall" into material and psychic substances, is split into two poles, one intellectual and the other existential: it is divided into intelligence and existence, into brain and body. In the Intellect intelligence is existence, and conversely; the distinction of aspects does not yet imply a scission. Scissions are produced only within the world of forms.

In other words the mind is the center of the body, whereas the Intellect is simultaneously the center of mind and body; but it is corporeal, of course, only insofar as it is the center of the body, which means insofar as it is heart. This is because mind and body both reflect the Intellect, or rather mind and body "are" the Intellect by bipolarized reflection within peripheral and shifting Existence; neither of the two could reflect the Intellect in a total way, their bipolarization being in short the sign of their remoteness with respect to their common source. It is thus that the reflection of the sun cannot exist without the water that receives it; water like the body is the receptacle of the ray, solar in the first case and intellectual in the second; it has itself a solar or luminous quality through its capacity for reverberation.

But this projection of the Intellect into the existential periphery not only results in a bipolarization into mind and body or inward ego and outward ego, but also in an opening of the mind by means of the faculties of sensation and action to the material world, in which the body is plunged. To speak of mind is to speak of both an intellectual center and a material periphery: while being of an intellectual substance, the mind is turned toward matter, the plane of crystallization, segmentation, and movement; it emanates from the Intellect and disperses itself in matter. As we have said, the mind is to the body what the Intellect is to the pairing mind-body; this pair is the Intellect bipolarized in view of matter or more precisely in view of sensible or sensory Existence. The heart and the brain, far from producing respectively the Intellect and the mind, are only their traces in the body, traces that are necessary by virtue of the body's "existential intellectuality".

*

*   *

The fundamental reason for the scission of the "exteriorized Intellect" is existential separation into "subject" and "object": whereas in the Intellect knowledge is being and being is knowledge, in peripheral Existence knowledge becomes mind, and being becomes body, without our being able to say however that the mind is "nonexistent" or the body "non-conscious"; on the other hand it is true that this polarity is prefigured in the Intellect, which itself also has an aspect of subject or "knowing" and an aspect of object or "being", and yet again an aspect of beatitude or "joy",[1] this joy becoming life in the earthly creature and uniting the ego-subject, mind, with the ego-object, body; but in the Intellect precisely these aspects, though distinguishable, are not separated, any more than are form, luminosity, and heat in the sun, although they may become separate on earth and from the terrestrial point of view.

---

[1] This is the Hindu *Trimûrti*, the "Triple Manifestation" of the universal Intellect (*Buddhi*): *Sat* (Being), *Chit* (Consciousness), *Ânanda* (Beatitude).

The Intellect in a certain sense is "divine" for the mind and "created" or "manifested" for God; it is nonetheless necessary to distinguish further between a "created Intellect" and an "uncreated Intellect", the second being the divine Light and the first the reflection of this Light at the center of Existence; "essentially" they are One, but "existentially" they are distinct, so that we could say in Hindu style that the Intellect is "neither divine nor non-divine", an elliptical expression which the Latin and Western mentality will doubtless balk at, but which transmits an essential shade of meaning. Be that as it may, when we speak of the Heart-Intellect we mean the universal faculty of which the human heart is for us the symbolic seat, but which, while being "crystallized" in accordance with the planes of reflection, is nonetheless "divine" in its single essence.

Every manifestation or creature is distinguished from the Principle or the Creator by an inversion of relationships, comparable to what we observe in every reflection;[2] a tree reflected in water is upside down, but it is still a tree, for the mirror changes the relationships but not the content;[3] now the manifested Intellect must itself also be distinguished by an inversion with regard to its non-manifested or divine Prototype. In fact, while everything is contained principially in the "Self", the universal Intellect is on the contrary the content as it were of the manifested Universe; it is the center or the heart of the world, whereas the divine Intellect is neither center nor periphery: it contains everything without being periphery, and it determines everything without being center; it "is real" in "knowing", and it "knows" in "being real".[4] The difference does not then concern intellectual absoluteness, but solely ontological "situation": the manifested Intellect, without ceasing to be "divine" in its essence, is nonetheless subject to cosmic objectification and thence to an indefinite diversity of lesser objectifications.

We have just said that the Intellect as such, whatever its metaphysical degree, is "divine" in essence; what we have said about the Intellect

---

[2] This is the law of "inverse analogy" presented by Guénon in his *Vedânta*.

[3] Nevertheless, to invert is to falsify. The world, while being truth through its content, is a "lie" with regard to God. God alone is truth.

[4] We put "being real" in place of "being" in order to avoid ontological restriction; in pure metaphysics God is not limited to Being; He is supra-personal while also being personal.

in divinis—namely, that there is within it no polarization—therefore also applies to the universal Intellect, not indeed insofar as it is manifest, but insofar as, being Intellect, it has the nature of Intellect.

The fact[5] that "everything is *Âtmâ*"—and this must in no way be taken in a pantheistic sense, things "being *Âtmâ*" to the extent they are distinct from nothingness and also through their symbolism, but not "in themselves"—is expressed by the ambiguity of what lies at the boundary of the cosmos or the Principle; we have seen that the Intellect is ambiguous because, while being "divine", it is also manifested, and the same applies to Being: though already "relative", it is still divine. The "line of demarcation" between God and the world can thus be thought of in different ways according to whether one is distinguishing between the ontological Principle and its creation, or between the universal Intellect and things, or again between the Absolute and the relative, the Real and the unreal, the Self and its objectifications, *Paramâtmâ* and *Mâyâ*; in this last case, which metaphysically is the most important and "most true", the "personal God"—Being—is found on "this side" of the "demarcation line", for He is already objectivized in relation to the absolute Subject, the Self, or rather He is the principial objectification, that from which all others result, though without "emanation", since Being is Principle; Being is "God", and yet it is already "relativity" or "lesser absoluteness" in relation to Beyond-Being.[6] On the other hand, when one distinguishes between the personal and creator God and the creation, the "line" in question separates the ontological Principle from its manifestation or Being from existences; hence it is situated "below" the "line" separating Reality and non-reality,[7] or the Absolute and the relative, or the Self and "illusion". Finally, when we distinguish between the Intellect and the ego—the ego being mental and corporeal—the "line of demarcation" between "Divine" and "created" crosses the actual "territory" of the created and is therefore situated "below" the preceding line. In other words Being is "ambiguous" because it is at the same

---

[5] The word "fact" has only a verbal function here, for it goes without saying that a principial reality is not a "fact".

[6] This is the Eckhartian distinction between *Gott* (God) and *Gottheit* (Godhead).

[7] Or "lesser reality", according to the point of view.

time absolute and relative or because it is absolute while being situated in relativity, or again—to express ourselves more boldly though perhaps all the more suggestively—because it is the "relative Absolute". In an analogous way, the Intellect is "ambiguous" because it is at the same time divine and human, uncreated and created, principial and manifested, which Being never is; the Intellect is "Principle manifest" whereas Being is "Principle determined" or "made relative", but always non-manifested. The ambiguity of the "partition" between the two great orders of Reality appears as if in one case manifestation had "encroached" on the Principle while in the other the Principle had "encroached" on manifestation.

*

* *

Looking at man from the outside, we can distinguish two formal elements, the body and the head, and we can say that each alike manifests a third element that is hidden, namely, the heart. The outward man is perfect to the extent that his face and body express the heart, not only by beauty but also, and indeed above all, by interiorization; this is what the sacred image of the Buddha conveys by the immutable majesty of the face with half-closed eyes and also by the symmetry and calm of the pose and by the gesture indicating silence, cessation, return to the center, contemplation: this is preeminently the image of the Heart-Intellect penetrating right into the body and absorbing it in its own infinitude. Spirituality, all things considered, is nothing other than the penetration of the mind-body by the Intellect, which as it were advances upon it, fills it, and transforms it for the sake of God; but it is also the return—not by "projection" this time, but by "absorption"—of the mind-body into the Intellect. This allows one to understand that the fundamental yogic posture—which the image of the Buddha transposes onto the plane of sacramental art—is derived from a veritable alchemy of forms and centers. Sometimes the Buddha is represented standing and sometimes lying on one side;[8] he is contemplative in action (upright position) as well as in non-action (seated

---

[8] The Koran teaches that God should be remembered "standing upright, seated, and lying on one side", which refers to the same symbolism.

79

position); his sleep is wakefulness, and his waking sleep (lying position). Sapiential sanctity is the sleep of the ego and the waking of the Self or Void; the moving surface of our being must sleep, for "I sleep, but my heart waketh." It is not disinterested activity that must sleep, but the life of the instincts, the passional comings and goings of the soul. Man's habitual dream lives in the past and the future: the soul is as if suspended in the past and at the same time swept along by the future instead of reposing in Being. God is "Being" in the absolute sense, that is, insofar as He is Essence and not determination or movement; He loves what is in conformity with Being, so that in the soul it is the aspect "being" that He loves above all; this aspect joins with that of "consciousness", and this amounts to saying that to return to our "being" is to realize pure "consciousness". God loves our actions only insofar as they are expressions of our "being" or ways toward it; our activity in itself is without importance.

The ternary "heart-brain-body"—or "Intellect-mind-body"—is prefigured in the ternary "Self-Spirit-World": just as the divine Spirit—universal Intellect—and the macrocosm, of which it is the luminous and celestial center, together constitute a bipolarized projection of the Self in "existential nothingness", so too the mind and the body it illumines and directs project the Intellect into the existential periphery, which is the realm of alternations; and just as the Self is "absent" from manifestation as such, which covers it like a veil while of necessity also expressing it—for "to exist" is "to express"—so too the heart is hidden in man while head and body, mind-intelligence and body-existence, are outwardly visible. The heart is to head and body what the Self is to the Spirit and man. If "the Word is made flesh", it is because the Heart-Intellect has penetrated all the way into the corporeal night in order to reintegrate "projected" or "separated" existence into the unity and peace of pure Being.

Love of God, Consciousness of the Real

Love seems to be the only element capable of uniting the soul to God, for it alone is desire of possession or union—a desire whose sublimation can engender the greatest sacrifices—whereas knowledge, as seen from this point of view, appears on the contrary as a static element having no operative or unitive virtue. To adopt this standpoint is either a question of terminology—and then "knowledge" is taken to mean only theory while "love" is held to exclude no mode of spiritual union—or it shows a misconception of metaphysical "consciousness", which is an eminently concrete participation in transcendent realities: far from denying love or the fear that is its complement, this consciousness embraces them in surpassing them, and because it surpasses them.[1] Before being able to "love" it is necessary to "be conscious"; the sun pours out light before heat, as is proven by the visibility of immeasurably distant stars; and to be conscious in the sense that interests us here is to fix the heart in the Real, in permanent "remembering" of the Divine. Fear distances from the world, and love brings near to God; but consciousness "is" already something of its content or aim; it is true that this observation is valid for other spiritual modes as well, but in a less direct way since intellective consciousness alone transcends human subjectivity by definition. In a certain sense love saves because

---

[1] "The word 'incantation' . . . must be understood as referring essentially to an aspiration of the being toward the Universal with the object of obtaining an inner illumination, whatever may be the outward means . . . that can be employed as accessory supports of the inward act, and which have as their effect the production of rhythmic vibrations causing a repercussion throughout the indefinite series of states of the being" (René Guénon, *L'Homme et son devenir selon le Vedânta*, Chapter 20, note). "And indeed many examples are to be met with in the *Veda* of persons who have neglected to carry out such rites . . . or who have been prevented from doing so, and yet, by maintaining their attention perpetually concentrated and fixed on the Supreme *Brahma* (in which consists the one and only really indispensable preparation), have acquired true Knowledge concerning It" (*L'Homme et son devenir*, Chapter 22). In all this it is indeed a matter of "aspiration", "inner act", and "concentrated attention", but without there being a question of "love" in the direct sense of the term.

it includes the whole subject, whereas consciousness delivers because it excludes it.[2]

Within the framework of *gnosis*, love has something impersonal about it because the love of man for God joins in a sense with that of God for man. The divine quality of "love" is everywhere, being in the very substance of the Universe, "created by love"; it belongs to no single person and embraces all; it is derived in short from the supreme Beatitude, which is at the same time divine Contemplation and creative Will.

All men have the need in some degree or another to understand and to love; but there are men who understand only love and act through it alone, just as there are others who are stirred only by sapiential consciousness; the element "truth" then takes precedence over the element "life", if one may so express it. The fundamental contemplation of these souls—and not the sharpness of their intelligence on lower planes—is equivalent to a need for total truth and cannot be stopped by formal screens, any more than light can come to rest in space; for these screens, being symbols, are transparent, only the blind believing them to be opaque. Contemplativity implies furthermore a certain natural distance with regard to the world, not only because things appear in their metaphysical "translucence"—outward alternatives then lose much of their importance—but also because the human world is shown up in all its absurdity, so that the simple fact of enduring it is already a form of asceticism.

*

* *

The fact that the term "love" evokes above all the ideas of sexual attraction and family affection indicates that it is not arbitrary to attribute to the way of love a character of emotiveness, even sentimentalism; but the term is necessarily broadened once it becomes the common denominator of all spirituality for an entire tradition. Now it is precisely the idea of "union"—included in the notion of love—that allows us to give the name of "love" to whatever attaches us to God

---

[2] This is not unrelated to the phonetic resemblance of the Latin words *amor* and *mors*. Love, which includes everything, is a sort of death, and death, which excludes everything, is like losing consciousness in love.

in an effective way; no matter our motives, we "love" the place we wish to be, the object we want to possess, the state we wish to enjoy. In this sense we can accept without hesitation the postulate of the preeminence of "love" over a "knowledge" that remains mental and inoperative.

Love thus divested of its emotive aspect—but not of its character of "union", lest the word lose all its meaning—is none other, all things considered, than the will: in fact the will obeys intellectual as well as sentimental motives; it is neutral in itself, but never operates alone, its motive always coming from outside; but from another angle the will allows itself to become absorbed by what determines it and thus becomes as it were an aspect of the driving intention.

When Christ—in renewing the Law of Sinai, which he came to "fulfill" and not to "destroy"—teaches the love of God,[3] he distinguishes between "heart", "soul", "strength" (*Torah*: "might"), and "mind"; this "love" thus excludes no faculty that unites with God, and it cannot be merely one term of an opposition, as when love and knowledge confront each other. If by the word "love" the *Torah* and the Gospel express above all the idea of "union" or "desire for union", they make it clear by the adjectives that follow that this tendency includes diverse modes in keeping with the diversity of man's nature; hence it is necessary to say, not that love alone draws toward God, but rather that only what draws toward God is love.

*

*   *

Love, even when considered in its current sense and in its psychological specificity, readily goes hand in hand with a desire to suffer for the Beloved, for it burns to be able to prove its fullness.[4] Metaphysical consciousness, on the other hand, carries its dimensions within itself: the detachment it implies is not really distinct from it, and this is why it does not impose itself as a suffering or sacrifice, but only insofar as it

---

[3] Deuteronomy 6:5 and 10:12; Matthew 22:37; Mark 12:30; Luke 10:27.

[4] This is obvious in the case of woman when one considers the pangs of childbirth; now love of the creature for the Creator is necessarily a "feminine" love since we are passive in the face of what determines us.

is a "void", a "poverty", or an "extinction" for the sake of the plenitude of the Self.

There is all the same a mystical love which does not necessarily lead to suffering and which, more contemplative than volitive, is connected to beauty; the condition of this love is a vision of the "metaphysical transparency" of things and so also—by compensation—a detachment with regard to them, which means that this love is akin to *gnosis*. This connection between love and beauty—which appears with special significance in the sexual realm—permits one to conceive of a love that responds to the Beauty of God and of a Mercy that responds to the beauty of human virtues or, in a deeper sense, to the beauty of the divine virtues as reflected in man.[5]

It is this connection moreover that permits in principle the integration of pleasure into spirituality, even if only to the extent this is inevitable. It is necessary to distinguish here between contingent level and absolute content or between the aspect of "manifestation" and that of "revelation"; the first is animal or "worldly" and the second spiritual. The demiurgic tendency moves away from God—from the macrocosmic point of view—but with a creative and revelatory intention, and this second characteristic allows the microcosm to return to God through the medium of the symbol; the satanic tendency, on the contrary, separates from God and so is opposed to Him; however, the very least of insects is obedient to Heaven by its subjection to natural laws as much as by its form. The devil's greatest vexation is that he is obliged to be a symbol of God, doubtless inverted, but always recognizable and ineffaceable.

*

* *

---

[5] This mysticism of beauty is more oriental than western and more contemplative than volitive; we find it in men like Saint Bernard and Saint Francis of Assisi as well as in Fra Angelico, not forgetting the troubadours and the *Fedeli d'Amore*, with whom it seems to have given rise to an alchemy with erotic symbolism, akin perhaps to a certain tantrism. Let us also mention, in relation to Judeo-Christianity, the symbolism of the Song of Songs and, in a much more general sense, the function at once aesthetic and spiritual of the liturgy. In Islam "the Beautiful" (*al-Jamîl*) is a divine Name, and the virtues are sometimes called "beauties" (*husnâ*).

The consciousness of which we have spoken has as it were two faces, one turned toward the Absolute and the other toward relativities: just as it is impossible to love God without also loving one's neighbor and without hating the world and the ego, so too consciousness of the Self and its initial objectifications demands and brings with it consciousness of cosmic structures, whether of the macrocosm or the microcosm.

To be conscious of the Self is to know first of all—and we cannot express what words cannot contain—that we are not really ourselves except beyond our empirical ego, that this ego is foreign to our innermost reality, which belongs not to us but we to it, although the ego reflects this reality in its own way and on its own level; it is also to know in a correlative fashion that God is All-Reality, that the world is "nothing"—otherwise it would be infinite and eternal—and that we ourselves are "nothing" in relation to our first Cause: that the world is in God but that God is not of this world.

In the cosmic order consciousness necessarily approaches the perspectives of fear and love for the simple reason that the situation of our ego in the Universe could not appear to us in a "neutral" way. To be conscious of death and Judgment is to approach a "wisdom of fear" whether one likes it or not; for the individual as such cannot like dying, unless it is to escape evils that appear even greater, and above all he cannot remain indifferent to the idea of the beyond, given that "God alone is good" and that there is in principle little chance that the generality of ordinary mortals will have nothing to fear from the divine "Hand of Rigor". In an analogous though different sense—and there is no analogy without diversity—to be conscious of the divine Mercy is to enter into the universal ray of love; for it is necessarily to turn toward God with hope and joy, as is also the case for consciousness of the real Presence of the Divine, into which we pass having as it were exited space and time in order to find again the pure essence of all we can love here below.

Seeing God Everywhere

One often hears it said that it is necessary to "see God everywhere" or "in everything"; this does not seem a difficult conception for men who believe in God, though there are many degrees involved, extending from simple reverie to intellectual intuition. How can one attempt to "see God", who is invisible and infinite, in what is visible and finite without the risk of deluding oneself or falling into error or without giving the idea a meaning so vague that the words lose all significance? This is the question we propose to clarify here, though it means returning to certain points we have already treated elsewhere.

First of all it is necessary to consider in the things around us—as well as in our own soul to the extent it is an object of our intelligence—what might be called the "miracle of existence". Existence indeed partakes of the miraculous: it is through existence that things are so to speak detached from nothingness; the distance between them and nothingness is infinite, and seen from this angle the least speck of dust possesses something of the absolute, hence of the "divine". To say that one must see God everywhere means above all that one must see Him in the existence of beings and things, our own included.

But phenomena do not have existence alone, or else they would not be distinct; they also have qualities that are superimposed as it were on existence and deploy its virtualities. The quality distinguishing a good thing from a bad resembles on a lesser scale the existence distinguishing each thing from nothingness;[1] as a consequence positive qualities represent God, as does existence pure and simple. Beings are attracted by qualities because they are attracted by God; every quality or virtue, whether the slightest of physical properties or the most profound of human virtues, transmits to us something of the divine

---

[1] We speak here of nothingness as if it had some reality, which is metaphysically necessary in certain cases even though logically absurd. If there is no nothingness, there is nevertheless a "principle of nothingness", but a principle which—since nothingness does not exist—always stops halfway. This principle is like the inverted shadow of the infinitude of Beyond-Being; it is *Mâyâ*, which is illusorily detached from *Âtmâ* without being able to emerge from *Âtmâ* and still less to abolish it.

Perfection, which is its immutable source, so that metaphysically speaking we can have no other motive for love than this Perfection.

But there is yet another "dimension" to be considered by the man who seeks the remembrance of God in things. The enjoyment that qualities afford us shows that they not only exist around us, but also concern us personally by way of Providence; for a landscape that exists without our being able to see it is one thing, and a landscape we can see is another. There is thus a "subjective-temporal" dimension, which is added to the "objective-spatial" dimension, if one may express it this way: things recall God to us not only to the extent they are good or display an aspect of goodness, but also to the extent we can perceive this goodness or enjoy it in a direct way. In the air that we breathe and that might be denied us, we meet God in the sense that the divine Giver is in the gift. This manner of "seeing God" in his gifts corresponds to "thanksgiving" while the perception of qualities corresponds to "praise"; as for the "vision" of God in mere existence, this gives birth in the soul to a general or fundamental consciousness of the divine Reality.

Thus God reveals himself not only by the existence and qualities of things, but by the gift He makes of them to us; He reveals himself also by contraries, that is, by the limitation of things and by their defects,[2] and again by the absence or disappearance of something which, being good, is useful and agreeable to us. It will be noticed that the concrete opposite of existence is not nothingness—which is only an abstraction—but limitation, which itself prevents existence from extending to pure Being, hence from becoming God. Things are limited in multiple ways, but above all by their existential determinations, which on the terrestrial level are matter, form, number, space, time. A clear distinction must be made between the aspect "limit" and the aspect "defect"; indeed the ugliness of a creature is not of the same order as the spatial limitation of a perfect body, for this limitation expresses a form, a normative principle, or a symbol whereas the ugliness corresponds only to a lack and does nothing but confuse the clarity of the symbolism. Be that as it may, what God reveals by the limitation of things, by their defects, and also—in relation to the human subject—by the

---

[2] It is in this sense that Meister Eckhart could say: "The more he blasphemes, the more he praises God."

privation of things or of qualities is the "non-divine", hence "illusory" or "unreal", character of all that is not He.

*

*   *

All things are only the accidentalities of a unique and universal substance, Existence, which remains always virgin in relation to its productions; it manifests, but is not itself manifested; that is to say, it is the divine act, the creative act, which starting from Being produces the totality of creatures. Hence it is Existence that is real and not things, substance not accidents, the unvarying not the variations. Since this is so, how could things not be limited, and how could they not proclaim by their multiple limitations the uniqueness of the divine Word and thereby of God? For universal Substance is none other than the creative Word, the word "Be!", from which all things spring.

To speak of "existing" is to speak of "having qualities", but it is also to speak of "having limitations", even defects. We have already noted that things are limited not only in themselves, but also in relation to us; they are limited and ephemeral, and at the same time they elude our grasp, whether by their remoteness in space or by the destiny that carries them away. This again allows us to "see God in everything", for if God manifests His Reality, Plenitude, and Presence in giving, He manifests our relativity, our emptiness, and our absence—in relation to Him—in removing, that is, in taking back what He had given.

Just as qualities express existence on the level of existence itself, so do limitations express in an opposite sense the metaphysical unreality of things. And here there is a new manner of "seeing God everywhere": for each thing in existing is by that very fact "unreal" in relation to absolute Reality; hence it is necessary to discern in all things not only the existential aspects, but also the "nothingness" before God, or in other words the metaphysical unreality of the world. And it is existence[3] itself that furnishes us with the "substance" of this "nothing-

---

[3] Existence is positive and "divine" in relation to existing things and to the extent it is cause, but it is limitative and "demiurgic" in relation to God, who in creating limits Himself in a certain illusory sense, if such an expression is permitted; we speak of an illusory sense since God is immutable, impassible, unalterable.

ness": things are unreal or illusory in the very measure in which they become embedded in existence and to the extent their contact with the divine Spirit becomes thereby more and more indirect.

Quality, we have said, expresses existence on the level of existence itself; and we could say in an analogous way that a defect expresses limitation in a solely negative and accidental manner. For limitation stands in a certain manner between existence and nothingness: it is positive insofar as it delineates a form-symbol and negative insofar as it disfigures this form in seeking to bring it back, as it were, toward the indistinction of the essence, but "from below"; this is the classic confusion between the supra-formal and the formless, a confusion, let it be said in passing, which is the key to "abstract" and "surrealist" art. Nevertheless, although form has a positive function thanks to its power of expression, it at the same time limits what it expresses, which is an essence: the most beautiful body is like a congealed fragment of an ocean of inexpressible bliss.

*
*   *

To all these existential categories, subjective as well as objective, we can add those of symbolism. Although every phenomenon is inevitably a symbol since existence is essentially expression or reflection, it is necessary nonetheless to distinguish degrees of content and intelligibility: for example, there is a distinct—and not simply quantitative—difference between a direct symbol, such as the sun, and an indirect, quasi-accidental symbol; moreover there is the negative symbol, the intelligibility of which may be perfect, but whose content is dark, without forgetting the double meaning of many symbols, though not of those that are most direct. The science of symbols—not simply a knowledge of traditional symbols—proceeds from the qualitative meanings of substances, forms, spatial directions, numbers, natural phenomena, positions, relationships, movements, colors, and other properties or states of things; it is not a question here of subjective appreciations, for cosmic qualities are ordered toward Being and are in keeping with a hierarchy that is more real than the individual; hence they are independent of our tastes, or rather they determine those tastes to the extent we are ourselves conformed to Being; we assent to the qualities to the extent we are "qualitative".[4] Symbolism, whether it resides in nature or is affirmed in sacred art, also corresponds to a manner of "seeing God everywhere", provided this vision is spontaneous thanks to an intimate knowledge of the principles from which the science of symbols proceeds; this science coincides at a certain point with the "discerning of spirits", which it transposes on to the plane of forms or phenomena, whence its close connection with the art of traditional cultures.

"How" then do things symbolize God or "divine aspects"? One cannot say that God is this tree or that this tree is God, but one can say that in a certain connection the tree is not "other than God", or that it cannot not be God in any way since it is not nonexistent. For the tree has existence, then the life that distinguishes it from minerals, then its particular qualities that distinguish it from other plants, and finally its symbolism, all of which are for the tree so many ways not only of not "being nothingness", but also of affirming God in one or another respect: life, creation, majesty, axial immutability, or generosity.

In a certain sense God alone is "that which is not nothing"; He alone is "non-nonexistence"—two negatives at once, but having their precise function. Truths of this kind can give rise indirectly and by deviation to pantheism and idolatry, but this does not prevent them from being true or therefore from having legitimacy, to say the least, on their own level.

Symbolism would have no meaning if it were not a contingent, but always conscious, mode of the perception of Unity; for "seeing God everywhere" is perceiving above all the Unity—*Âtmâ*, the Self—in phenomena. According to the *Bhagavad Gîtâ* (18:20-22), "The knowledge that recognizes in all beings one unique, imperishable, indivisible essence, although scattered among separate objects, proceeds from *sattva*" (the tendency that is "luminous", "ascending", "conformed to Being", *Sat*); and the same text continues: "But the knowledge which, led astray by the multiplicity of objects, sees in all beings diverse and

---

[4] A man must be quite perverse to see no qualitative-objective difference between what is noble and what is base, unless he places himself at the transcendent point of view of the non-differentiation of *Âtmâ*, which is an absolutely different thing from a subversive and iconoclastic egalitarianism. Be that as it may, it is this science of qualitative phenomena that permits one to situate the aberrations of contemporary art with an implacable justice and to rend the veil of its false mystery.

distinct entities proceeds from *rajas* (the 'fiery' and 'expansive' tendency). As for the shortsighted knowledge which, without returning to causes, is attached to a particular object as if it were all, this proceeds from *tamas*" (the "dark" and "descending" tendency). It is necessary here to take into account the angle from which things are considered: the cosmic tendencies (*gunas*) are not only in the mind of man, but clearly enter as well into his faculties of relative knowledge and into the realms that correspond to them, so that reason can no more escape diversity than can the eye; further, to say that a given form of knowledge "recognizes a unique essence in all beings" amounts to affirming that these beings exist on their own plane. It is a question then of admitting not that there are no objective differences around us, but that these differences are in no way opposed to the perception of the unity of the essence; the "passional" perspective (*rajas*) is not at fault because it perceives differences, but because it lends them an absolute character as if each being were a separate existence; this the eye does as well in a certain manner precisely because it corresponds existentially to a "passional" view to the extent it belongs to the ego, which is "made of passion". The Intellect, which perceives the unity of essence in things, discerns at the same time the differences of modes and degrees as a function of this unity, for otherwise there would be no distinction among the *gunas*.

*

*   *

We have alluded above to the conditions of sensible or psychophysical existence: space, time, form, number, substance—modes, it may be added, which are not all reducible to our plane of existence, since this plane cannot be a closed system, any more than they enclose man entirely, since man opens out toward the Infinite. These conditions denote so many principles allowing one to "see God in things": space extends and conserves while limiting by form; time limits and devours while extending by duration; form both expresses and limits; number is a principle of expansion but without a qualitative power, or without formal virtue, if one prefers; finally substance, which on the physical plane becomes "matter",[5] denotes existence on a given level,

---

[5] This fifth condition has sometimes been called "life", undoubtedly to express the

hence the "level of existence".[6] Form, which in itself is qualitative, has something quantitative about it when it is material; number, which in itself is quantitative, has something qualitative when it is abstract. The materiality of form adds size to form, hence a quantity; the symbolic character of number frees it from its quantitative function and confers upon it a principial value, hence a quality.[7] Time, which is as if "vertical" in relation to "horizontal" space—if one may risk introducing a geometrical symbolism into a consideration which, precisely, goes beyond the spatial condition—thus surpasses terrestrial existence and is projected in a certain fashion and within certain limits into the "beyond", something already hinted at in terrestrial life by the connection between psychic life and time; this connection is more intimate than that linking the soul with the space surrounding us, as is shown by the fact that it is easier to abstract oneself in concentration from spatial extension than from duration; the soul of a blind man is as it were cut off from space, but not from time. As for matter, it is—even more directly than animic or subtle substance—universal substance "congealed"[8] or "crystallized" by the cold proximity of "nothingness"; the process of manifestation could never reach this "nothingness" for

---

idea that inertia cannot be absolute or that ether possesses a certain vital potentiality, without which life—"breath" (or *prâna*)—would find no receptacle.

[6] The Sanskrit word for "matter", *bhûta*, includes the meaning of "substance" or "subsistence"; matter is derived from substance, being a reflection of it on the plane of "gross" coagulation, and is connected through substance with Being.

[7] This is number in the Pythagorean sense, of which the universal rather than the quantitative import is already to be divined in geometrical figures; the triangle and the square are "personalities" and not quantities, essentials and not accidentals. Whereas one obtains ordinary number by addition, qualitative number results on the contrary from an internal or intrinsic differentiation of principial unity; it is not added to anything and does not depart from unity. Geometrical figures are so many images of unity; they exclude one another, or rather they denote different principial qualities: the triangle is harmony, the square stability; these are "concentric" not "serial" numbers.

[8] This "congealing" does not affect substance itself any more than, in the order of the five elements, "solidification"—or the diversification of the elements in general—affects the ether, which subsists within them. All the same this comparison is not adequate since ether is an element and is therefore not located on another plane, despite its "central" position and "virginity", whereas universal substance is transcendent in relation to its productions.

the simple reason that an absolute "nothing" does not exist, or rather exists only by virtue of the "indication", "direction", or "tendency" in the creative work itself; we see an image of this in the fact that cold is only a privation and thus has no positive reality even though it transforms water into snow and ice as if it had the power to produce bodies.

Space "sets out" from the point or the center; it is "expansion", and it "tends"—without ever being able to attain it—toward infinitude; time sets out from the instant or the present;[9] it is duration, and it tends toward eternity; form sets out from simplicity; it is differentiation or complexity, and it tends toward perfection; number sets out from unity; it is multiplicity or quantity, and it tends toward totality;[10] finally matter sets out from ether; it is crystallization or density, and it tends toward immutability, which is at the same time indestructibility. In each of these cases, the "middle term"—what the respective condition "is"—seeks fundamentally the perfection or virtue of the "point of departure", but it seeks it on its own level or rather in its own movement where it is impossible to attain it: if expansion had the virtue of the point, it would be infinity; if duration had the virtue of the instant, it would be eternity; if form had the virtue of simplicity, it would be perfection; if number had the virtue of unity, it would be totality; if matter had the virtue—unalterable because omnipresent—of ether, it would be immutability.

If it is objected that perfection on the formal plane is attained by the sphere, we reply that formal perfection cannot be restricted to

---

[9] In relation to the "point" and the "instant", the "center" and the "present" denote a perspective at once qualitative and subjective: a qualitative subjectivity, because the subject is the Self. The objective terms "point" and "instant" certainly imply this same "quality", but the spiritual relationship—not the metaphysical relationship—is less direct and less apparent precisely because the respective notions are cut off from life.

[10] In these two conditions, form and number, the respective points of departure—simplicity and unity—have a concrete existence, doubtless because these conditions are "contents" in relation to space and time, which are "containers"; on the other hand, the points of departure of these latter conditions—the point and the instant—have respectively neither extent nor duration. Nevertheless, spherical simplicity is not one form among others since it is incomparable, any more than unity is a quantity properly speaking since it is not added to anything; if there were only simplicity and unity, there would be neither form nor number.

the simplest form, for what distinguishes a beautiful form of complex character—such as the human body—from the sphere is not at all a lack of perfection, the less so since the formal principle tends precisely toward complexity; it is only therein that it can realize beauty. But this in no way signifies that perfection can be attained on this plane; in fact complex perfection would demand a form combining the most rigorous necessity or intelligibility with the greatest diversity, and this is impossible because formal possibilities are innumerable to the very extent they move away from the initial spherical form by means of differentiation. In plunging into complexity, one can attain the "unilateral" or "relatively absolute" perfection of a given beauty, certainly, but not the integral and absolute perfection of all beauty; the condition of pure necessity is realized only in the spherical and "undifferentiated" proto-form.

What enters into space enters also into time; what enters into form enters also into number; what enters into matter thereby enters into form, number, space, time. Space, which "contains" like a matrix[11] and "preserves", recalls Goodness or Mercy; it is connected with love. Time for its part ceaselessly throws us into a "past" that is no more and carries us toward a "future" that is not yet, or rather will never be, and that we do not know save for death, the sole certainty of life—which implies that time is associated with Rigor or Justice and is connected with fear. As for matter, it recalls Reality to us, for it is the mode of "non-nonexistence" everywhere apparent to us, in our body just as in the sight of the Milky Way; form reminds us of the divine Law or universal norm, for it is either veridical or erroneous, exact or false, essential or accidental; finally number unfolds before us the limitlessness of All-Possibility, "countless" like the sands of the desert or the stars of the sky.

However much space may limit its contents, it cannot prevent them from existing; and however much time may prolong its contents, they will one day cease to exist all the same. Duration does not abolish ephemerality any more than spatial limitation abolishes extension. In space nothing is ever wholly lost; in time all is irremediably lost.

Existence is manifested *a priori* by substance. Substance has two containers, space and time, of which the first is positive and the

---

[11] It is for us like a "womb of immortality", death being birth into eternal Life.

second negative; it has also two modes, form and number, of which the first is limitative and the second expansive. Number reflects space since it extends; form reflects time since it restricts.

If a man could live a thousand years, he would doubtless end by feeling himself crushed by the limits of things—hence also by space, time, form, number, matter—but in compensation he would see in contents only essences. A child or indeed an ordinary man sees on the contrary only contents, at once without essences and without limits.

*
* *

Each of these conditions of our earthly existence has two "openings" toward God: space includes the geometric point or the "center" on the one hand and limitless extension, the "infinite", on the other; likewise time includes the instant or the "present" as well as indefinite duration, "eternity"; in space we are as it were between the center and the infinite and in time between the present and eternity, these being so many dwellings of God that take us out of the two "existential dimensions"; we cannot prevent ourselves from thinking of them when we are conscious of these conditions in which we live and which so to speak live in us. The center and the infinite, the present and eternity, are respectively the poles of the conditions of space and time, and yet we at the same time escape these conditions by these very poles: the center is no longer in space, strictly speaking, any more than the geometric point has extension, and the absolute present or the pure instant is no longer in duration: as for the infinite, it is a kind of "non-space" as eternity is "non-time".

Let us now consider the formal condition: there is in this case geometric perfection and bodily perfection, and both reveal God; the Creator manifests Himself in the "absoluteness" of the circle, the square, the cross just as in the beauty—the "infinity"—of man or a flower; geometric beauty is "cold", bodily beauty "warm". But strictly speaking the "center" of the formal condition is the void; elementary geometrical forms, starting with the sphere, are only the first "issuings forth" of form out of the void, hence at the same time its first "expressions" and "negations". The sphere is the form that remains nearest the void, whence its perfection of simplicity; the human body in its normative beauty—and the varied modes it comprises—is what approaches most nearly to plenitude, which corresponds to the oppo-site perfection, that of complexity. Plenitude is what brings together a maximum of homogeneous aspects or introduces totality into form: the sphere and man correspond in formal mode to unity and totality; what number expresses in an abstract, separative, and quantitative mode, form expresses in a concrete, unitive, and qualitative mode. Zero is to unity what the void is to the sphere; unity denotes God whereas totality is equivalent to His manifestation, the cosmos.

*
*   *

"Seeing God everywhere" is seeing Oneself (*Âtmâ*) in everything; it is being conscious of the analogical correspondences—insofar as they are "modes of identity"—between the principles or possibilities which, included first in the divine Nature, expand or reverberate "in the direction of nothingness" and constitute the microcosm as well as the macrocosm, of which they create at one and the same time the receptacles and the contents. Space and time are receptacles; form and number appear as contents, although they are containers in relation to the substances they coagulate or divide into segments. Matter is in a more visible way both container and content at the same time; it "contains" things and "fills" space; its contents are eaten away and devoured by time, but it itself remains quasi-timeless so that it coincides with the whole of duration.

The problem of time is intimately linked with that of the soul and can give rise to the following question: what meaning must be given to the dogmatic doctrine of the soul held by Monotheists, according to which the soul is said to have no end while having had a begin-ning? The metaphysical absurdity of an eternity created in time or of a purely "unilateral" perpetuity is obvious; but since theological orthodoxy excludes absurdity pure and simple, one must seek beyond the words and in symbolism for the explanation of a doctrine that is so contradictory. Let us say at once that Monotheism includes in its perspective only what is of direct interest to man, so that it appears as a "spiritual nationalism" of mankind; but since the state preceding our terrestrial birth was as little human as are the animal and angelic states, it is treated as nonexistent, exactly as are the souls of animals and plants; we are therefore called "soul" only from the moment of our human birth or rather from our entry into the womb. But there is something else of much more importance; the temporal creation of the soul—that is, its entry into the human state—expresses our relativity; by contrast the celestial perpetuity of the soul or its eternity with God concerns its absolute side, the "uncreated" quality of its essence; we are at once relative and absolute, and this fundamental paradox of our being explains what is illogical or "mysterious" about the very formulation of the theological doctrine of the soul. It must not be forgotten, on the other hand, that *creatio ex nihilo* affirms above all a divine causality in contrast to an ever threatening "naturalism"; and to say that the soul is "eternal" can only mean on the level of absolute truth that it is "essentially" the Self.

*
* *

The faculty of "seeing God in everything" can be independent of all intellectual analysis; it can be a grace, the modes of which are imponderables and which springs from a profound love of God. When we say "intellectual analysis", we do not at all mean speculations in the void; the "categories" of which we have spoken are by no means "abstract", but their perception clearly depends on a discernment which appears to be abstract from the point of view of sensations and which, though far from delighting in sterile dissections, is nevertheless obliged to "separate" in order to "unite". Separation and union alike are in the nature of things—each on its own level, if one can express it this way; the eye, the better to see a mountain, needs a certain distance: this distance reveals differences, it permits visual analysis, but at the same time it "unites" or synthesizes in furnishing an adequate and total image of the mountain.

To see God everywhere and in everything is to see infinity in things, whereas human animality sees only the surface and relativity; it is to see at the same time the relativity of the categories in which man moves and which he believes to be absolute. To see the infinite in the finite is to see that this flower before us is eternal because an eternal spring is affirmed through its fragile smile; to see relativity is to grasp that this instant we are living is not "now", that it "is past" even before it has arrived, and that if time could be stopped, with all beings remaining fixed as in a river of ice, the human masquerade would appear in all its sinister unreality; all would seem absurd save only the "remembrance of God", which is situated in the immutable.

To see God everywhere is essentially this: to see that we are not, that He alone is. If from a certain point of view humility can be called the greatest of the virtues, this is because it implies in the final analysis the cessation of egoity and for no other reason. One could say as much—with only a small change of perspective—about each fundamental virtue: perfect charity is to lose oneself for God, for one cannot lose oneself in God without in addition giving oneself to men. If love of neighbor is fundamental on the strictly human plane, it is not only because the "neighbor" is finally the "Self" as are "we", but also because this human charity—or this projection into the "other"—is the only means possible for the majority of men of detaching themselves from the "I"; it is less difficult to project the ego into "the other" than to lose it for God, although the two things are indissolubly linked.

*
* *

Our form is the ego: it is the mysterious incapacity to be other than oneself and at the same time the incapacity to be entirely oneself and not "other-than-Self". But our Reality does not leave us the choice and obliges us to "become what we are" or remain what we are not. The ego is empirically a dream in which we ourselves dream ourselves; the contents of this dream, drawn from our surroundings, are at bottom only pretexts, for the ego desires only its own life: whatever we may dream, our dream is always only a symbol for the ego, which wishes to affirm itself, a mirror which we hold before the "I" and which reverberates its life in multiple fashions. This dream has become our second nature; it is woven of images and tendencies, static and dynamic elements in innumerable combinations: the images come from outside and are integrated into our substance, whereas the tendencies are our responses to the world around us; as we exteriorize ourselves, we create a world in the image of our dream, and the dream thus objectified flows back upon us, and so on and on until we are enclosed in a tissue, sometimes inextricable, of dreams exteriorized or materialized and of materializations interiorized. The ego is like a watermill whose wheel, under the pressure of a current—the world and life—turns and repeats itself untiringly in a series of images always different and always similar.

The world: it is as if the "conscious Substance" that is the Self had fallen into a state that would split it up in multiple ways, inflicting upon it an infinity of accidents and infirmities; the ego is in fact ignorance floundering in objective modes of ignorance, such as time and space. What is time if not ignorance of what will be "after", and what is space if not ignorance of what escapes our senses? If we were "pure consciousness" like the Self, we would be "always" and "everywhere", which means that we would not be "I", for in its empirical actuality this "I" is entirely a creation of space and time. The ego is ignorance of what is the "other"; our entire existence is woven of ignorances; we are like the Self frozen, then hurled "to earth" and broken into a thousand fragments; we observe the limits surrounding us, and we conclude that we are fragments of consciousness and of being. Matter grips us like a kind of paralysis, imposing on us the heaviness of a mineral and exposing us to the miseries of impurity and mortality; form shapes us according to a particular model, imposing on us such and such a mask and cutting us off from a whole to which we are none the less linked, though at death it lets us fall as a tree gives up its fruit; finally, number is what repeats us—within us as around us—and it is what in repeating us diversifies us, for two things can never be absolutely identical; number repeats form as if by magic, and form diversifies number and must thus create itself ever anew, for All-Possibility is infinite and must manifest its infinitude. But the ego is not only multiple outwardly in the diversity of souls; it is also divided within itself in the diversity of tendencies and thoughts, which is not the least of our miseries; for "strait is the gate", and "a rich man shall hardly enter into the kingdom of heaven".

And since "we are not other" than the Self, we are condemned to eternity. Eternity lies in wait for us, and this is why we must again find the Center, the place where eternity is beatitude. Hell is the reply to the periphery that makes itself Center or to the multitude that usurps the glory of Unity; it is the reply of Reality to the ego that wishes to be absolute and that is condemned to be so without being able to be so. The Center is the Self "freed", or rather what has never ceased to be free—eternally free.

III

CHRISTIANITY

Some Observations

In the perspective of *gnosis*, Christ, "Light of the world", is the universal Intellect, as the Word is the "Wisdom of the Father". Christ is the Intellect of microcosms as well as that of the macrocosm; he is thus the Intellect in us[1] as well as the Intellect in the Universe and *a fortiori* in God; in this sense it can be said that there is no truth or wisdom that does not come from Christ, and this is obviously independent of all consideration of time and place.[2] Just as "the Light shineth in darkness; and the darkness comprehended it not", so too the Intellect shines in the darkness of passions and illusions. The relationship of the Son to the Father is analogous to the relationship of pure Love to Being or of the Intellect to the "Self", and this is why in the Intellect or in sanctifying Grace we are "brothers" of Christ.

But Christ is likewise prefigured in the whole creation, and this has an aspect of incarnation and another of crucifixion. On a lesser scale humanity, and with it the individual human, is an image of Christ and includes both aspects: man is "incarnation" by his Intellect and freedom and "crucifixion" by his miseries.

*

* *

---

[1] The Word "was the true Light, which lighteth every man" (John 1:9).

[2] "Now faith," says Saint Paul, "is the substance of things hoped for, the evidence of things not seen. . . . Through faith we understand that the worlds were framed by the word of God, so that things which are seen were not made of things which do appear" (Hebrews 11:1, 3); this proves that faith is, to say the least, not contrary to *gnosis*; doubtless not all faith is metaphysical knowledge, but all metaphysical knowledge, being an "evidence of things not seen", is of the domain of faith. *Gnosis* is the perfection of faith in the sense that it combines this knowledge with the corresponding realization; it is wisdom and sanctity: sanctifying wisdom and sapiential sanctity. The most external expression of the element "realization" is works, which on the one hand prove and on the other hand give life to faith, and without which it is "dead, being alone" (James 2:17).

From the doctrinal point of view Christian *gnosis* is nothing other than Trinitarian metaphysics,[3] with its microcosmic application: our pure existence corresponds to the Father, our pure intelligence to the Son, and our pure will to the Holy Spirit. The vertical line of the cross denotes the relationship of the Father to the Son, whereas the horizontal line symbolizes the Holy Spirit; the latter "proceeds from the Father and is delegated by the Son", which signifies that the Spirit, being at once Beatitude and Will, proceeds from the Father, then also from the Son (*Filioque*) insofar as he represents the Father, but not insofar as he is distinct from Him. The Father is Beyond-Being, the Son is Being, and the Spirit is Beatitude and Manifestation; when the perspective is limited to ontology, the Father is Being as such and the Son the "Consciousness" of Being. To say that the Spirit is Beatitude and Manifestation—whatever the level of the perspective, ontological or supra-ontological—means that it is at once the "inner life" and the "creative projection" of Divinity: it is thus an "expansion" or "spiration" *in divinis* at the same time as a "springing forth" *ex divinis*; it is on the one hand "internal" or "contemplative" Beatitude and on the other hand "external" or "active" Beatitude. This is why in the sign of the cross the Holy Spirit "occupies" the whole of the horizontal line; it could even be said that in the making of this sign the words *Spiritus Sanctus* designate the Spirit *in divinis* and the word *Amen* the Spirit "in creation", if one may venture such an expression.

The Spirit "as creation" is none other than the Virgin in three aspects, macrocosmic, microcosmic, and historical: it is Universal Substance, then the soul in a state of sanctifying grace, and finally the human manifestation of these aspects, the Virgin Mary. In this sense we could say that the word *Amen* is a name of the Virgin, perfect creature—or perfect creation—and that if the vertical line of the sign of the cross denotes the relationship of the Father and the Son, the horizontal line will denote the relationship of Husband and Spouse. The entire soul of the Virgin is one great *Amen*; there is nothing in it which is not an acquiescence to the Will of God.

---

[3] In a generally analogous way, the metaphysics of Islam is unitary in the sense that it proceeds by principial reductions to Unity, whereas the metaphysics of Judaism is at once unitary and denary (Decalogue, *Sephiroth*).

*

* *

Christian art includes essentially three images: the Virgin and Child, the Crucifixion, and the Holy Face: the first image is related to the Incarnation, the second to the Redemption, and the third to the Divinity of Christ. Man recapitulates these three symbols or mysteries respectively by purity, which is the vehicle of "Christ in us", by death to the world, and by sanctity or wisdom.

Strictly speaking, art forms part of the liturgy—in the broadest sense—for like the liturgy it is "public work" (λειτουργία);[4] this being so one cannot leave it to the arbitrary disposition of men. Art, like the liturgy properly so called, constitutes the terrestrial "garment" of God; it both envelops and unveils the divine Presence on earth.[5]

*

* *

The Church of Peter is visible and is continuous like water; that of John—instituted on Calvary and confirmed at the sea of Tiberias—is invisible and is discontinuous like fire. John became "brother" of Christ and "son" of the Virgin, and he is moreover the Prophet of the Apocalypse; Peter is charged to "feed my sheep", but his Church seems to have inherited also his denials, whence the Renaissance and its direct and indirect consequences; nevertheless, "the gates of hell

---

[4] According to Saint Augustine, the liturgy is essentially simple, so that this simplicity is almost a criterion of authenticity; if it were otherwise, says the Bishop of Hippo, the liturgy would be lower than the Jewish Law, which was itself given by God and not by liturgists; furthermore he stresses the fact that Christian feasts are few in number.

[5] We have had occasion at various times to underline the sacred, hence immutable, character of religious art: it is not a purely human thing, and above all it does not consist in seeking impossible mysteries in nonexistent profundities, as is the intention of modern art, which, instead of adapting "our times" to the truth, aims at adapting the truth to "our times". In relation to artistic or artisanal—hence "liturgical"—expression, the terms "Christian" and "medieval" are in fact synonymous; to repudiate Christian art on the pretext that Christianity stands above "cultures" is a failure to see the context and value of this art; it is to repudiate elements of truth and thereby also of sanctity.

shall not prevail against it". John "tarries till I come", and this mystery remains closed to Peter;[6] there is here a prefiguration of the "schism" between Rome and Byzantium. "Feed my sheep": there is nothing in these words that excludes the interpretation put upon them by the Greeks, according to which the Bishop of Rome is *primus inter pares* and not *pontifex maximus*.

*

*   *

The Holy Spirit is given by Confirmation through the medium of fire, for oil is none other than a form of liquid fire, as is wine; the difference between Baptism and Confirmation could be defined by saying that the first has a negative—or "negatively positive"—function since it "takes away" the state of the fall, whereas the second sacrament has a purely positive function in the sense that it "gives" a light and a power that are divine.[7]

This transmission acquires a new "dimension" and receives its full efficacy through the vows that correspond to the "Evangelical counsels"; these vows—true initiatic leaven—denote at the same time a death and a second birth, and they are in fact accompanied by symbolic funeral rites; the consecration of a monk is a sort of burial.[8] By

---

[6] It is significant that the Celtic Church, that mysterious springtime world appearing like a sort of last prolongation of the golden age, held itself to be attached to Saint John.

[7] According to Tertullian, "The flesh is anointed that the soul may be sanctified; the flesh is signed that the soul may be fortified; the flesh is placed in shadow by the laying on of hands that the soul may be illumined by the Holy Spirit." As for Baptism, the same author says that "the flesh is washed that the soul may be purified". According to Saint Dionysius, Baptism, Eucharist, and Confirmation refer respectively to the ways of "purification", "illumination", and "perfection"; according to others, it is Baptism which is called an "illumination"; this clearly does not contradict the foregoing perspective since all initiation "illumines" by definition: the taking away of "original sin" opens the way to a "light" preexisting in Edenic man.

[8] These funeral rites make one think of the symbolic cremation which, in India, inaugurates the state of *sannyâsa*.

poverty man severs himself from the world; by chastity he severs himself from society; and by obedience he severs himself from himself.[9]

*

*   *

The whole of Christianity hangs on these words: Christ is God. Likewise on the sacramental plane: the bread "is" his body, and the wine "is" his blood.[10] There is furthermore a connection between the Eucharistic and onomatological mysteries: the Named one is "really present" in his Name; that is to say, he "is" his Name.

The Eucharist is in a sense the "central" means of grace in Christianity; it must therefore express integrally what characterizes this tradition, and it does so by recapitulating not only the Christic mystery as such, but also its double application to the "greater" and the "lesser" mysteries: the wine corresponds to the first and the bread to the second, and this is indicated not only by the respective natures of the sacred elements, but also by the following symbolic facts: the miracle of the bread is "quantitative" in the sense that Christ multiplied what already existed, whereas the miracle of the wine is "qualitative", for Christ conferred on the water a quality it did not have, namely, that of wine. Or again: the body of the crucified Redeemer had to be pierced in order that blood might flow out; blood thus represents the inner aspect of the sacrifice, which is moreover underscored by the fact that blood is liquid, hence "non-formal", whereas the body is solid, hence "formal"; the body of Christ had to be pierced because, to use the language of Meister Eckhart, "if you want the kernel, you must break the shell". The water that flowed from Christ's side and proved his death is like the negative aspect of the transmuted soul: it is the "extinction" which, depending on the point of view, either accompanies or pre-

---

[9] The married man can be chaste "in spirit and in truth", and the same necessarily holds good for poverty and obedience, as is proved by the example of Saint Louis and other canonized monarchs. The reservation expressed by the words "in spirit and in truth", or by the Pauline formulation "the letter killeth, but the spirit giveth life", has a capital importance in the Christian perspective, but it also contains—moreover providentially—a "two-edged sword".

[10] For Clement of Alexandria, the body of Christ—or Eucharistic bread—concerns active life or faith, and the blood or the wine contemplation and *gnosis*.

cedes the beatific plenitude of the divine blood; it is the "death" which precedes "Life" and which is as it were its outward proof.

*

* *

Christianity hangs also on the two supreme commandments, which contain "all the law and the prophets". In *gnosis* the first commandment—total love of God—implies taking hold of the consciousness of the Self, whereas the second—love of neighbor—refers to seeing the Self in what is "not-I". Likewise for the injunctions of *oratio et jejunium*: all Christianity depends on these two disciplines, "prayer and fasting".

Oratio et jejunium: "fasting" is first of all abstention from evil and then the "void for God"—*vacare Deo*—a void in which "prayer", the "remembrance of God", is established and which is filled by the victory already won by the Redeemer.

"Prayer" culminates in a constant recalling of divine Names insofar as it is a question of an articulated "remembrance". The *Golden Legend*, so rich in precious teachings, contains stories that bear witness to this: a knight wished to renounce the world and entered the Cistercian order; he was illiterate and moreover incapable of retaining from all the teachings he received anything but the words *Ave Maria*; these words "he kept with such great recollectedness that he pronounced them unceasingly wherever he went and whatever he was doing". After his death a beautiful lily grew on his grave and on each petal was written in golden letters *Ave Maria*; the monks opened the grave and saw that the root of the lily was growing from the knight's mouth. To this story we have only one word to add concerning the "divine quality" of the Name of the Virgin: he who says Jesus says God; and in the same way he who says Mary says Jesus, so that the *Ave Maria*—or the Name of Mary—is of the divine Names the one which is closest to man.

The *Golden Legend* recounts also that the executioners of Saint Ignatius of Antioch were astonished by the fact that the saint pronounced the Name of Christ without ceasing: "I cannot keep from doing so," he told them, "for it is written in my heart." After the saint's death, the pagans opened his heart and there saw, written in golden letters, the Name of Jesus.[11]

*

*   *

God is Love just as He is Light, but He is also sacrifice and suffering in Christ, and this too is an aspect or extension of Love. Christ has two natures, divine and human, and he also offers two ways, *gnosis* and charity: the way of charity, to the extent it is distinguished from *gnosis*, implies pain, for perfect love desires to suffer; it is in suffering that man best proves his love; but there is as it were a price to be paid for the "intellectual easiness" of such a perspective. In the way of *gnosis*, where the whole emphasis is on pure contemplation and the chief concern is with the glorious aspect of Christ rather than with his grievous humanity—and where there is in certain respects a participation in the divine nature, ever blissful and immutable—suffering does not apply in the same way, which means that it does not in principle have to exceed the demands of a general *ascesis*, such as the Gospel designates by the term *jejunium*; a quasi-impersonal detachment here takes precedence over an individual desire for sacrifice. All Christian spirituality oscillates between these two poles, although the aspect

---

[11] The same fact is recounted of a Dominican saint, Catherine dei Ricci. Apart from the *Ave Maria* and the Name of Jesus, let us mention as well the double invocation *Jesu Maria*, which contains as it were two mystical dimensions, as also the *Christe eleison*, which is in effect an abridgement of the "Jesus Prayer" of the Christian East; it is known that the mystical science of ejaculatory prayer was transmitted to the West by Cassian, who appears retrospectively as the providential intermediary between the two great branches of Christian spirituality, while in his own time he was for the West the representative of the mystical tradition as such. And let us also recall here these liturgical words: *Panem celestem accipiam et nomen Domini invocabo* and *Calicem salutaris accipiam et nomen Domini invocabo*. In Greek and Slavic monasteries, a knotted rope forms part of the investiture of the Small Schema and the Great Schema; this rope is ritually conferred on the monk or nun. The Superior takes this rosary in his left-hand and says: "Take, brother N., the sword of the Spirit, which is the word of God, to pray to Jesus without ceasing, for you must constantly have the Name of the Lord Jesus in the mind, in the heart, and on the lips, saying: 'Lord Jesus Christ, Son of God, have mercy on me, a sinner.'" In the same order of ideas, we would draw attention to the "act of love"—the perpetual prayer of the heart—revealed in our times to Sister Consolata of Testona (see *Un appel du Christ au monde* by Lorenzo Sales).

109

charity-suffering greatly preponderates in practice—and for obvious reasons—over the aspect *gnosis*-contemplation.

In the soul of the gnostic, the question "What is God?" or "What am I?" outweighs the question "What does God want of me?" or "What must I do?", although these questions are far from precluded since man is always man. The gnostic, who sees God "everywhere and nowhere", does not base himself in the first place on outward alternatives even though he cannot escape them; what matters to him above all is that the world is everywhere woven of the same existential qualities and poses in all circumstances the same problems of remoteness and proximity.

*

* *

The emphasis in the Christian climate on the virtue of humility—or rather the mode of the emphasis or the virtue—leads us to return to this issue, which is at once moral and mystical.[12]

Humility has two aspects, which are prefigured in the Gospel by the washing of the feet on the one hand and the cry of abandonment on the cross on the other. The first humility is effacement: when we are brought, rightly or wrongly, to see a quality in ourselves, we must first attribute it to God and secondly see in ourselves either the limits of this quality or the defects that could neutralize it; and when we are brought to see a defect in others, we must first try to find its trace or the responsibility for it in ourselves and secondly exert ourselves to discover qualities that can compensate for it. But truth—provided it is within our reach—surpasses every other value, so that to submit to truth is the best way to be humble; virtue is good because it is true, and not conversely. Christ humbled himself in washing the feet of his disciples; he abased himself by serving while he was yet the Master, but not by calumniating himself; he did not say: "I am worse than you," and he gave no example of virtue contrary to truth or intelligence.[13]

---

[12] We have already spoken of it toward the end of our *Perspectives spirituelles et faits humains.*

[13] Christ gave other teachings on humility, for example when he said that he had not come to be served but to serve or when he said that "whosoever therefore

The second—the great—humility is spiritual death, the "losing of life" for God, the extinction of the ego; this is what saints have had in view in describing themselves as "the greatest of sinners"; if this expression has a meaning, it applies to the ego as such, and not to such and such an ego. Since all sin comes from the ego and since without it there would be no sin, it is indeed the ego that is the "most vile" or the "lowest of sinners"; when the contemplative has identified his "I" with the principle of individuation, he perceives as it were in himself the root of all sin and the very principle of evil; it is as if he had assumed, after the example of Christ, all our imperfections in order to dissolve them in himself in the light of God and in the burnings of love. For a Saint Benedict or a Saint Bernard, the "degrees of humility" are stages in the extinction of the passional "I", stages marked by symbols-attitudes, by disciplines that further the transmutation of the soul; the key to this wisdom is that Christ was humbled on the cross through identifying himself in the night of abandonment with the night of the human ego and not through identifying himself with a given "I"; he felt himself forsaken not because he was Jesus, but because he had become man as such; he had to cease being Jesus that he might taste all the straitness, all the separation from God, of the pure ego and thereby of our state of fall.[14]

shall humble himself as this little child, the same is greatest in the kingdom of heaven"; now the true nature of all children is purity and simplicity, not rivalry. Let us recall also the parable of the uppermost rooms at feasts. According to Saint Thomas Aquinas, humility demands neither that we should submit what is divine in us to what is divine in another, nor that we should submit what is human in us to what is human in another, nor still less that the divine should submit to the human; but there is still the question, sometimes delicate but never insoluble, of the proper definition of things.

[14] The saying of Christ: "Why callest thou me good? There is none good but one, that is, God" refers to the greater humility that is in question here; it is the same when Christ cites little children as examples. If it were necessary to take literally the mystical conviction of being the "vilest of sinners", one would not be able to explain how saints who have had this conviction could speak about the evil of some heretic; moreover it would be absurd to ask men to have an acute sense of the least defects of their nature and at the same time to be incapable of discerning these defects in another.

That we may not be able to determine our place in the hierarchy of sinners by no means signifies that we do not have the certitude of being "vile", not only as ego in general, but thereby also as a particular ego; to believe oneself "vile" for the sole reason that one is "I" would empty humility of its content.

Humility in Christianity is conceived as a function of love, and this is one of the factors conferring upon it its characteristic texture. "The love of God," says Saint Augustine, "comprises all the virtues."

*
* *

"And the Light shineth in darkness; and the darkness comprehended it not." By its form the message of Christ is addressed *a priori* to the passional element in man, to the point of fall in human nature, while remaining gnostic or sapiential in Christ himself and therefore in Trinitarian metaphysics, to say nothing of the sapiential symbolism of Christ's teachings and parables. But it is in relation to the general form—the volitive perspective—of the message that Christ could say: "They that are whole have no need of the physician, but they that are sick: I came not to call the righteous, but sinners to repentance" (Mark 2:17). In the same way when Christ says: "Judge not, that ye be not judged," he is referring to our passional nature and not to pure intelligence, which is neutral and is identified with those "that are whole". If Christ shall come to "judge the quick and the dead", this again relates to the Intellect—which alone has the right to judge—and to the equation "Christ-Intellect".

The volitive perspective we have just alluded to is affirmed in the clearest possible way in Biblical history: we see there a people at once passionate and mystical, struggling in the grip of a Law that crushes and fascinates them, and this prefigures in a providential way the struggles of the passional soul—of every soul to the extent it is subject to passions—with the truth, which is the final end of the human state. The Bible always speaks of "what happens" and almost never of "what is"; the Cabalists tell us that it does the latter implicitly, which we are the first to recognize, but this changes nothing in the visible nature of these Scriptures nor in the human causes of this nature. From another angle Judaism had hidden what Christianity was called upon to make openly manifest;[15] on the other hand the Jews had openly manifested from the moral point of view what Christians later learned to hide; the ancient coarseness was no doubt replaced by an esoterism of love, but also by a new hypocrisy.

It is necessary to take account of this as well: the volitive perspective has a tendency to retain the ego because of the idea of moral responsibility, whereas *gnosis* tends on the contrary to reduce it to the cosmic powers of which it is a combination and a conclusion. And again: from the point of view of will and passion, men are equal; but they are not so from the point of view of pure intellection, for intellection introduces into man an element of the absolute, which as such transcends him infinitely. To the moralizing question: "Who art thou that judgest another?"—a question by which some would like to obliterate all "wisdom of serpents" or all "discerning of spirits" in a vague and charitable psychologism—one would have the right in every case of infallible judgment to reply, "God"; for intelligence, insofar as it is "relatively absolute", escapes the jurisdiction of virtue, and therefore its rights surpass those of man regarded as passional and fallible ego; God is in the truth of every truth. The saying that "no one can be judge and party in his own cause" can be applied to the ego to the extent it limits or darkens the mind, for it is arbitrary to attribute to the intelligence as such a fundamental limit in connection with an order of contingencies; to assert as certain moralists would that man has no right to judge amounts to saying that he has no intelligence, that he is only will or passion, and that he has no kind of likeness to God.

The sacred rights of the Intellect appear moreover in the fact that Christians have not been able to dispense with Platonic wisdom and that later the Latins felt the need for recourse to Aristotelianism, as if thereby recognizing that *religio* could not do without the sapiential element, which a too exclusive perspective of love had allowed to fall into disrepute.[16] But if knowledge is a profound need of the human spirit, it is by this very fact also a way.

---

[15] Commentators on the *Torah* state that the impediment of speech from which Moses suffered was imposed on him by God so that he would not be able to divulge the Mysteries which, precisely, the Law of Sinai had to veil and not unveil; now these Mysteries were at root none other than the "Christic" Mysteries.

[16] The ancient tendency to reduce *sophia* to a "philosophy", that is, an "art for art's sake" or a "knowledge without love", hence a pseudo-wisdom, has necessitated the

To return to our earlier thought, we could also express ourselves this way: contrary to what is the case in *gnosis*, love scarcely has the right to judge another; it takes everything upon itself and excuses everything, at least on the plane where it is active, a plane whose limits vary according to individual natures; "pious fraud"[17]—out of charity—is the price of volitive individualism. If *gnosis* for its part discerns essentially—and on all levels—both spirits and values, this is because its point of view is never personal, so that in *gnosis* the distinction between "I" and "other" and the subtle and paradoxical prejudices attaching to it scarcely have meaning; but here too the application of the principle depends on the limitations imposed on us by the nature of things and by our own nature.

Charity with regard to our neighbor, when it is the act of a direct consciousness and not just a moral sentiment, implies seeing ourselves in the other and the other in ourselves; the scission between *ego* and *alter* must be overcome in order that the division between Heaven and earth may be healed.

*
*   *

According to Saint Thomas, it is not in the nature of free will to choose evil, although this choice comes from having freedom of agency connected with a fallible creature. Will and liberty are thus joined together, which means that the Doctor introduces into the will an

predominance in Christianity of the contrary viewpoint. Love in the sapiential perspective is the element that surpasses simple ratiocination and makes knowledge effective; this cannot be emphasized enough.

[17] Veracity, which in the end has more importance than moral conjectures, implies in short the use of logic in a manner that is consequential, that is, putting nothing above the truth, not falling into the contrary fault of believing that to be impartial means not to consider anyone right or wrong. One must not stifle discernment for the sake of impartiality, for objectivity does not consist in absolving the wrong and accusing the good, but in seeing things as they are, whether this pleases us or not; it is therefore to have a sense of proportion as much as a sense of shades of meaning. It would be pointless to say such elementary things if one did not meet at every turn this false virtue, which distorts the exact vision of facts and which could dispense with its scruples if only it realized sufficiently the value and efficacy of humility before God.

intellectual element and makes the will participate, quite properly, in intelligence. Will does not cease to be will by choosing evil—we have said this on other occasions—but it ceases fundamentally to be free, hence intellective; in the first case it is the dynamic faculty, passional power—animals also have a will—and in the second the stimulation of discernment. It could be added that neither does intelligence cease to be itself when in error, but in this case the relationship is less direct than for the will; the Holy Spirit (Will, Love) is "delegated" by the Son (Intellect, Knowledge), and not conversely.

Christian doctrine does not claim that moral effort produces metaphysical knowledge, but it does teach that restoring the fallen will—extirpating the passions—releases the contemplativity latent in the depths of our theomorphic nature; this contemplativity is like an aperture that divine Light cannot but accede to, whether as Justice or *a fortiori* as Mercy; in *gnosis* this process of mystical alchemy is accompanied by appropriate concepts and states of consciousness.[18] Seen from this angle, the primacy of love is not opposed to the perspective of wisdom, but illumines its operative aspect.[19]

---

[18] Knowledge is then "sanctifying" and is not limited to satisfying some more or less justifiable need for explanation; it accords fully with the Pauline doctrine of charity. The implacability of such knowledge is not arrogance, but purity. *Gnosis* makes of knowledge something effective, ontological, "lived". Outside of *gnosis* it is not a question of extirpating the passions, but of directing them toward Heaven.

[19] The Augustinian-Platonic doctrine of knowledge is still in perfect accord with *gnosis*, while Thomistic-Aristotelian sensationalism, without being false on its own level and within its own limits, is in accord with the demands of the way of love in the specific sense of the term *bhakti*. But this reservation is far from applying to the whole of Thomism, which is identified in many respects with truth unqualified. It is necessary to reject the opinion of those who believe that Thomism, or any other ancient wisdom, has an effective value only when we "re-create it in ourselves"—we "men of today"!—and that if Saint Thomas had read Descartes, Kant, and the philosophers of the nineteenth and twentieth centuries, he would have expressed himself differently; in reality he would then only have had to refute a thousand more errors. If an ancient saying is right, there is nothing to do but accept it; if it is false, there is no reason to take notice of it; but to want to "rethink" it through a veil of new errors or impressions quite clearly has no interest, and any such attempt merely shows the degree to which the sense of intrinsic and timeless truth has been lost.

*

*   *

The morality that offers the other cheek—so far as morality can here be spoken of—does not mean an unwonted solicitude toward one's adversary, but complete indifference toward the fetters of this world, or more precisely a refusal to let oneself be caught up in the vicious circle of terrestrial causations; whoever wants to be right on the personal plane at any price loses serenity and moves away from the "one thing needful"; the affairs of this world bring with them only disturbances, and disturbances take one further from God. But peace, like every spiritual attitude, can dissociate itself from outward activity; holy anger is inwardly calm, and the unavoidable role of the office of judge—unavoidable because motivated by higher and non-personal interests—is compatible with a mind free from attachment and hatred. Christ opposes the passions and personal interest, but not the performance of duty or the collective interest; in other words he is opposed to personal interest when that interest is passionate or harmful to the interests of others, and he condemns hatred even when it serves a higher interest.

The "non-violence" advocated by the Gospels symbolizes—and renders effective—the virtue of the mind preoccupied with "what is" rather than with "what happens". As a rule man loses much time and energy in questioning himself about the injustice of his fellows as well as about possible hardships of destiny; whether there is human injustice or divine punishment, the world—the "current of forms" or "cosmic wheel"—is what it is, simply following its course; it is true to its own nature. Men cannot not be unjust insofar as they form part of this current; to be detached from the current and to act contrary to the logic of facts and the bondage it engenders is bound to appear madness in the eyes of the world, but it is in reality to adopt here below the point of view of eternity. And to adopt this point of view is to see oneself from a great distance: it is to see that we ourselves form a part of this world of injustice, and this is one more reason for remaining indifferent amid the uproar of human quarrelling. The saint is the man who acts as if he had died and returned to life; having already ceased to be "himself" in the earthly sense, he has absolutely no intention of returning to that dream, but maintains himself in a kind of wakefulness, which the world with its narrowness and impurities cannot understand.

Pure love is not of this world of oppositions; it is by origin celestial, and its end is God; it lives as it were in itself, by its own light and in the beam of God-Love, and this is why charity "seeketh not her own, is not easily provoked, thinketh no evil; rejoiceth not in iniquity, but rejoiceth in the truth; beareth all things, believeth all things, hopeth all things, endureth all things" (1 Corinthians 13:5-7).

Christic and Virginal Mysteries

God became man that man might become God. The first mystery is the Incarnation, and the second the Redemption.

However, just as the Word in assuming flesh was already in a sense crucified, so too man in returning to God must participate in both mysteries: the ego is crucified in relation to the world, but saving grace is made incarnate in the heart; sanctity is the birth and life of Christ in us.

This mystery of the Incarnation has two aspects: the Word on the one hand and its human receptacle on the other: Christ and the Virgin-Mother. In order to realize this mystery in itself, the soul must be like the Virgin, for just as the sun can be reflected in water only when it is calm, so the soul can receive Christ only in virginal purity, in original simplicity, and not in sin, which is turmoil and disequilibrium.

By "mystery" we do not mean something incomprehensible in principle—unless on the purely rational level—but something that opens on to the Infinite or is envisaged in this respect, so that intelligibility becomes limitless and humanly inexhaustible. A mystery is always "something of God".

*

* *

Ave Maria gratia plena, Dominus tecum: benedicta tu in mulieribus, et benedictus fructus ventris tui, Jesus.[1]

Maria is the purity, beauty, goodness, and humility of the cosmic Substance; the microcosmic reflection of this Substance is the soul in a state of grace. The soul in a state of baptismal grace corresponds to the

---

[1] "The devotion of the Rosary . . . is, when correctly grasped, as ancient as the Church. It is the appropriate devotion of Christians. It serves to revive and maintain the spirit and life of Christianity. The novelty of the Name can offend only those who do not know its real meaning: and Saint Dominic, who is regarded as the Author of this devotion, is in effect only its Restorer" (*La solide Dévotion du Rosaire*, by an unknown Dominican of the beginning of the eighteenth century).

Virgin Mary; the blessing of the Virgin is on him who purifies his soul for God. This purity—the Marian state—is the essential condition not only for the reception of the sacraments, but also for the spiritual actualization of the real Presence of the Word. By the word *ave* the soul expresses the idea that, by conforming to the perfection of Substance, it places itself at the same time into harmony with it, while imploring the help of the Virgin Mary, who personifies this perfection.

Gratia plena: primordial Substance, by reason of its purity, its goodness, and its beauty, is filled with the divine Presence. It is pure because it contains nothing other than God; it is good because it compensates and absorbs all forms of cosmic disequilibrium, for it is totality and therefore equilibrium; it is beautiful because it is totally submissive to God. It is thus that the soul, the microcosmic reflection of Substance—corrupted by the fall—must again become pure, good, and beautiful.

Dominus tecum: this Substance is not only filled with the divine Presence in an ontological or existential manner, in the sense that it is impregnated with it by definition, that is, by its very nature, but it is also constantly communicating with the Word as such. Thus if *gratia plena* means that the divine Mystery is immanent in the Substance as such, *Dominus tecum* signifies that God in His metacosmic transcendence is revealed to the Substance, just as the eye, which is filled with light, sees in addition the sun itself. The soul filled with grace will see God.

Benedicta tu in mulieribus: compared with all secondary substances, the total Substance alone is perfect and totally under divine Grace. All substances are derived from it by an abrogation of equilibrium; likewise all fallen souls are derived from the primordial soul through the fall. The soul in a state of grace—the soul pure, good, and beautiful—rejoins primordial perfection; it is thereby "blessed among all" microcosmic substances.

Et benedictus fructus ventris tui, Jesus: what in principle is *Dominus tecum* becomes in manifestation *fructus ventris tui, Jesus*; that is, the Word, which communicates with the ever-virgin substance of the total Creation, is reflected in an inverse sense within this Creation: it will appear as the fruit, the result, not as the root, the cause. And in the same way: the soul submissive to God by its purity, its goodness, and its beauty seems to give birth to God according to appearances; but God, being thus born in it, will transmute and absorb it, as Christ transmutes and absorbs his mystical body, the Church, which from being militant and suffering becomes triumphant. But in reality the Word is not born in the Substance, for the Word is immutable; it is the Substance that dies in the Word. Similarly, when God seems to germinate in the soul, it is in reality the soul that dies in God. *Benedictus*: the Word that becomes incarnate is itself Benediction; nevertheless, since according to appearances it is manifested as Substance, as soul, it is called blessed; for it is then envisaged not with respect to its transcendence—which would render Substance unreal—but with respect to its appearance, its Incarnation: *fructus*.

Jesus: it is the Word that determines Substance and reveals itself to it. Macrocosmically, it is the Word that manifests itself in the Universe as the divine Spirit; microcosmically, it is the Real Presence, affirming itself at the center of the soul, spreading outward, and finally transmuting and absorbing it.[2]

*
* *

The virginal perfections are purity, beauty, goodness, and humility; these are the qualities the soul in quest of God must realize.

Purity: the soul is empty of all desire. Every natural movement that asserts itself in the soul is then considered in relation to its passional quality in its aspect of concupiscence and seduction. This perfection is cold, hard, and transparent like diamond. It is immortality that excludes all corruption.

Beauty: the beauty of the Virgin expresses divine Peace. It is in the perfect equilibrium of its possibilities that the universal Substance realizes its beauty. In this perfection the soul gives up all dissipation in order to repose in its own substantial, primordial, ontological perfection. We said above that the soul must be like a perfectly calm expanse of water; every natural movement of the soul will then appear as agitation, dissipation, distortion, hence as ugliness.

---

[2] This expression should not be taken quite literally any more than other expressions of union that we shall use in what follows; the essential here is to be conscious of "deification", whatever significance one may give this term.

Goodness: the mercy of the cosmic Substance consists in this: virgin in relation to its productions, it contains an inexhaustible power of equilibrium, of recovery, of healing, of absorbing evil, and of manifesting good; maternal toward beings who address themselves to it, it in no way refuses them its assistance. Similarly, the soul must divert its love from the hardened ego and direct it toward the neighbor and the whole of creation; the distinction between "I" and "other" is as if abolished, the "I" becoming "other" and the "other" becoming "I". The passional distinction between "I" and "thou" is a death, comparable to the separation between the soul and God.

Humility: the Virgin, despite her supreme sanctity, remains woman and aspires to no other role; the humble soul is conscious of its own rank and effaces itself before what surpasses it. It is thus that the *Materia Prima* of the Universe remains on its own level and never seeks to appropriate to itself the transcendence of the Principle.

The joyful, sorrowful, and glorious mysteries of Mary are so many aspects of cosmic reality on the one hand and of the mystical life on the other.

Like Mary—and like universal Substance—the sanctified soul is "virgin", "spouse", and "mother".

*
*   *

The nature of Christ appears in four mysteries: incarnation, love, sacrifice, Divinity; and in these the human soul must participate in diverse ways.

The incarnation: this is manifested as a principle in every positive divine act, such as creation, or within creation in various divine affirmations, such as the Scriptures. In the soul it is the birth of the Divine—grace—but also transforming and salvific *gnosis*; it is also the divine act of prayer of the heart, the Name of God made incarnate in the soul as an invincible force. Christ as pure divine affirmation enters the world—and the soul—with the force of lightning, of the drawn sword; all natural imagery in the soul then appears as a passivity or indulgence toward the world, a forgetfulness of God resulting from weakness and negligence. In the soul the incarnation is the victorious—and ceaselessly renewed—presence of divine Miracle.

Love: God is love, infinite life. The ego on the contrary is a state of death, comparable in its congenital egoism to a stone and in its vain pettiness to sterile and shifting sand. The hardened heart must be liquefied: from being indifferent toward God, it must become fervent; but it will thereby become indifferent with regard to the ego and the world. The gift of tears is one manifestation of this liquefaction; spiritual intoxication is another.

Sacrifice: on the cross the annihilation of Christ attains its culminating point in the state of abandonment between Heaven and earth. It is thus that the ego must be annihilated in a perfect void before the exclusive Reality of God.

Divinity: what corresponds to this in the soul is pure spirituality, that is, permanent union with God. It is the remembrance of God, which must become the true center of our being in place of the illusory ego, which is dispersed among the appearances of this world below. The human person becomes perfectly "itself" only beyond itself, in profound and inexpressible Union.

*
* *

The Lord's Prayer is the most excellent prayer of all since it has Christ for its author; it is therefore more excellent as a prayer than the *Ave*, and this is why it is the first prayer of the Rosary. But the *Ave* is more excellent than the Lord's Prayer in that it contains the Name of Christ, which is mysteriously identified with Christ himself, for "God and His Name are identical"; now Christ is more than the Prayer he taught, and the *Ave*, which contains Christ through his Name, is thus more than this Prayer; this is why the recitations of the *Ave* are much more numerous than those of the *Pater* and why the *Ave* constitutes, with the Name of the Lord that it contains, the very substance of the Rosary. What we have just stated amounts to saying that the prayer of the "servant" addressed to the "Lord" corresponds to the "Lesser Mysteries"—and we recall that these concern the realization of the primordial or Edenic state, hence the fullness of the human state—whereas the Name of God itself corresponds to the "Greater Mysteries", the finality of which is beyond every individual state.

From the microcosmic point of view, as we have seen, "Mary" is the soul in a state of "sanctifying grace", qualified to receive the "Real

Presence"; "Jesus" is the divine Seed, the "Real Presence", which must bring about the transmutation of the soul, namely, its universalization or reintegration in the Eternal. "Mary"—like the "Lotus"—is "surface" or "horizontal"; "Jesus"—like the "Jewel"[3]—is "center" and, in dynamic relationship, "vertical". "Jesus" is God in us, God who penetrates and transfigures us.

Among the meditations of the Rosary the "joyful Mysteries" concern the "Real Presence" of the Divine in the human, from the point of view adopted here and in connection with ejaculatory prayers; as for the "sorrowful Mysteries" they describe the redemptive "imprisonment" of the Divine in the human, the inevitable profanation of the "Real Presence" by human limitations; finally the "glorious Mysteries" relate to the victory of the Divine over the human, the liberation of the soul by the Spirit.

---

[3] We are here alluding to the well-known Buddhist formula: *Om mani padme hum*. There is an analogy worth noticing between this formula and the name "Jesus of Nazareth": the literal meaning of *Nazareth* is "flower", and *mani padme* means "jewel in the lotus".

The Cross

If the Incarnation has the significance of a "descent" of God, Christ is thus equivalent to the whole of creation, containing it in a way; he is a second creation, which purifies and "redeems" the first. He assumes with the cross the evil of Existence; to be able to assume this evil, it was necessary that God should become Existence. The cross is everywhere because creation is necessarily separated from God; Existence affirms itself and blossoms out through enjoyment, but enjoyment becomes sin to the extent that God is not its object, although all enjoyment contains a metaphysical excuse in the fact that it is directed to God by its existential nature; every sin is broken at the foot of the cross. But man is not made solely of blind desire; he has received intelligence that he may know God; he must become conscious of the divine end in everything, and at the same time he must "take up the cross" and "offer the other cheek", which means he must rise even above the internal logic of the existential prison; his logic, which is "foolishness" in the eyes of the world, must transcend the plane of this prison: it must be "vertical" or celestial, not "horizontal" or earthly.

Existence or "manifestation" has two aspects: the tree and the cross; the joyful tree, which bears the serpent, and the sorrowful cross, which bears the Word made flesh. For the impious, Existence is a world of passion that man justifies by a philosophy "after the flesh"; for the elect, it is a world of trial transpierced by grace, faith, *gnosis*.

Jesus is not only the new Adam, but also the new Creation. The old is totality and circumference; the new, unicity and center.

*

* *

We can no more escape the cross than we can escape Existence. At the root of all that exists, there is the cross. The ego is a downward path that leads away from God; the cross is a halting of this path. If Existence is "something of God", it is also something "which is not God", and it is this that the ego embodies. The cross brings the latter back to the former and in so doing permits us to vanquish Existence.

What makes the problem of Existence so complex is that God shows through everywhere since nothing could exist outside Him; the whole object is never to be separated from this distant perception of the Divine. And this is why enjoyment in the shadow of the cross is conceivable and even inevitable; to exist is to enjoy, even though at the foot of the cross. This is where man must keep himself since such is the profound nature of things; man can violate this nature only in appearance. Suffering and death are none other than the cross reappearing in the cosmic flesh; Existence is a rose signed with a cross.

*
* *

Social morals distinguish between the rightness of one man and the wrongness of another; but the mystical morals of Christ, strictly speaking, admit no one to be right, or rather they are located on a plane where no one is entirely right since every man is a sinner, and "there is none good but one, that is, God."[1] The Mosaic Law has a man stoned for wronging society, an adulterer for example, but for Christ only God can be wronged, which excludes all forms of vengeance; every man is guilty before the Eternal. Every sin is that of Adam and Eve, and every human being is Adam or Eve;[2] the first act of justice will therefore be to forgive our neighbor. The fault of the "other" is at root our own; it is only a manifestation of the latent fault that constitutes our common substance.

But Christ, whose Kingdom is "not of this world", leaves open a door for human justice insofar as it is inevitable: "Render therefore unto Caesar the things which are Caesar's." To deny this justice on every plane would amount to setting up injustice; even so it is neces-

---

[1] "For I know nothing by myself; yet am I not hereby justified: but he that judgeth me is the Lord" (1 Corinthians 4:4).

[2] Saint Gregory the Great says in a letter—quoted by the Venerable Bede in his *Histoire de l'Eglise et du peuple anglais*—that "every sin proceeds from three causes, namely, suggestion, pleasure, and consent. Suggestion comes from the devil, pleasure from the body, and consent from the will. The serpent suggested the first sin, and Eve, as flesh, found in it a carnal pleasure whereas Adam, as mind, consented to it; but only the most subtle intelligence can distinguish between suggestion and pleasure and between pleasure and consent".

sary to overcome hatred by bringing evil back to its total root, to the "offence" that must needs come, but above all by discovering it in our nature, which is that of every ego; the ego is an optical illusion that makes a mote out of a beam and conversely, according to whether it is a question of "ourselves" or "another". It is necessary to find, through Truth, the serenity that understands all, "forgives all", and reduces all to equilibrium; it is necessary to vanquish evil with the peace that is beyond evil and hence not its contrary; true peace has no contrary.

"He that is without sin among you, let him first cast a stone": we are all of a same sinful substance, a same matter susceptible to the abscess that is evil, and we are therefore all joint partners in evil in a way that is doubtless indirect but nonetheless real; it is as if everyone carried in himself a particle of responsibility for all sin. Sin then appears as a cosmic accident, exactly like the ego on a larger scale; strictly speaking, he is without sin who is without ego and who is thereby like the wind, of which no man can "tell whence it cometh, and whither it goeth". If God alone has the right to punish, it is because He is beyond the ego; hatred means to arrogate to oneself the place of God, to forget one's human sharing of a common misery, to attribute to one's own "I" a kind of absoluteness, detaching it from that substance of which individuals are only so many contractions or knots. It is true that God sometimes delegates His right of punishment to man insofar as he rises above the "I", or must and can so rise; but to be the instrument of God is to be without hatred toward man. In hatred man forgets "original sin" and thereby burdens himself in a certain sense with the sin of the other; it is because we make ourselves God whenever we hate that we must love our enemies. To hate another is to forget that God alone is perfect and that God alone is Judge. In good logic one can hate only "in God" and "for God"; we must hate our ego, not the "immortal soul", and hate him who hates God to the extent he hates God and not otherwise, which amounts to saying that we should hate his hatred of God and not his soul.

Likewise, when Christ says it is necessary to "hate father and mother", this means that it is necessary to reject whatever in them is "against God", that is, the attachment that serves as an obstacle in regard to "the one thing needful". Such "hatred" implies a virtual liberation for those whom it concerns and is thus, on the plane of eschatological realities, an act of love.

*

*   *

"To take up the cross" is to keep oneself close to the existential cross: there is in Existence the pole "sin" and the pole "cross", the blind launching into enjoyment and the conscious stopping, the "broad way" and the "narrow way". "To take up the cross" is essentially not to "follow the crowd"; it is to "discern spirits", to keep oneself incorruptible in the apparent nothingness that is the Truth. "To take up the cross" means therefore to endure this nothingness, this threshold of God; and since the world is pride, egoism, passion, and false knowledge, it means to be humble and charitable, to "die" and become "as a little child". This nothingness is suffering to the extent we are pride and are thereby caused to suffer; the fire of purgatory is nothing else: it is our substance that burns, not because God wishes to hurt us, but because it is what it is—because it is "of this world" and in proportion to its being so.

*

*   *

The cross is the divine fissure through which Mercy flows from the Infinite.

The center of the cross, where the two dimensions intersect, is the mystery of forsakenness: it is the "spiritual moment" when the soul loses itself, when it "is no more" and when it "is not yet". Like the whole Passion of Christ, this cry is not only a mystery of grief in which man must share by renunciation, but also by contrast an "opening" that God alone can effect and did effect because He is God; and this is why "my yoke is easy, and my burden is light". The victory that devolves upon man has already been won by Jesus; for man nothing remains but to open himself to this victory, which thus becomes his own.

*

*   *

What is "abstraction" in the case of the logician becomes virtually corporeal in the case of the Word made flesh. The spear of the centurion Longinus has just pierced Christ's side; a drop of divine blood flowing down the spear touches the man's hand. At that moment the world collapses for him like a house of glass; the darkness of existence is torn away; his soul becomes like a weeping wound. He is as if drunk, but with a drunkenness that is cold and pure; all his life is henceforth like an echo repeating a thousand times that single instant at the foot of the cross. He has just been reborn, not because he has "understood" the Truth, but because the Truth has seized him existentially and torn him with a "concrete" gesture from this world. The Word made flesh is the Truth that has in a way become matter, but by that very fact a matter transfigured and new-minted, a matter that is burning light, transforming and delivering.

APPENDIX

Selections from Letters and
Other Previously Unpublished Writings

1

I must call your attention to an important aspect of universality or unity: the divergence between religions is not only due to the incomprehension of men; it is also in the Revelations, hence in the divine Will, and this is why there is a difference between exoterism and esoterism; the diverse dogmas contradict one another, not only in the minds of theologians, but also—and *a priori*—in the sacred Scriptures; in giving these Scriptures, however, God at the same time gives the keys for understanding their underlying unity. If all men were metaphysicians and contemplatives, a single Revelation might be enough; but since this is not how things are, the Absolute must reveal itself in different ways, and the metaphysical viewpoints from which these Revelations are derived—according to different logical needs and different spiritual temperaments—cannot but contradict one another on the plane of forms, somewhat as geometrical figures contradict each other as long as one has not grasped their spatial and symbolic homogeneity.

God could not wish for all men to understand Unity since this understanding is contrary to the nature of man in the "dark age". This is why I am against ecumenism, which is an impossibility and absurdity pure and simple. The great evil is not that men of different religions do not understand one other, but that too many men—due to the influence of the modern spirit—are no longer believers. If religious divergences are particularly painful in our times, this is only because the divisions between believers, in the face of an unbelief that has become more and more menacing, have become all the more acute and also all the more dangerous. It is therefore high time that: 1. men return to faith, whatever their religion may be, on condition that it is intrinsically orthodox and in spite of dogmatic ostracisms; 2. that those who are capable of understanding pure metaphysics, esoterism, and the inward unity of religions discover these truths and draw the necessary inward and outward conclusions. And this is why I write books.

2

It is altogether unfair to attribute to the Catholic Church alone the refusal to recognize the validity of other religions. There is no religion that recognizes equivalent traditions outside itself, and it is "materially" impossible, so to speak, that such a religion could exist, for how and in what form would it recognize other traditions? Would it do so by means of a criteriology or enumeration? Neither could be realized in practice.

Every religion is "a dogmatic authority with the mission of teaching faith and morals"; Catholicism did not need the Council of Trent for that.

That the Church condemned Meister Eckhart is no more astonishing than the fact that the *'ulamâ'* condemned al-Hallaj. If *gnosis* was suppressed in the West, this is no more the fault of the Church than that of the Western race. The Church's attitude reflects the lack of aptitude Europeans have for pure metaphysics.

As for Angelus Silesius, one must not forget that his *Cherubinischer Wandersmann* was published with the assent of the Church; and yet one finds there the boldest and most purely "jnanic" formulations.

One could never affirm that "esoterism is not subject to any external criteria"; if the sacraments have an esoteric character, this results on the contrary from their nature and dogmatic definition, at least with respect to Baptism, Confirmation, and "Communion".

The compliments made by ecclesiastical authorities today toward other religions proves absolutely nothing from the universalist point of view. It merely proves that the truth is put aside and that doctrinal rigor is replaced with a saccharine and democratic fog of "good will".

A refusal to recognize other religions is not a part of "it must needs be that offences come". "Go ye therefore, and teach all nations," Christ said. Recognition of other forms is never more than an intellectual and spiritual accident. We are no longer living in the *Krita-Yuga*, and Christ knew this. But if we accidentally have a knowledge belonging to the spirit of the *Krita-Yuga*, it is certainly not Christ who will oppose himself to it, and he will not be the one to ask us to give account of this knowledge to creatures of the *Kali-Yuga*, be they even theologians. It is not for nothing that he spoke of "pearls and swine". We owe an account to God alone for our metaphysical and universalist ideas.

3

The deepest nature of man—and thus the most real—is consciousness of God; it is for this that he was created. There is an outward man and an inward man; the first is submerged by sensory impressions, and the second is turned toward God: toward God who is the true Self of man.

It is said that in Heaven man enjoys the beatific vision, which is another expression for God-consciousness. Man can already participate in this vision here on earth precisely through the divine consciousness that is accessible to him and whose supports are the supreme Truth and the divine Name. It is in the invocation, illumined by the supreme Truth, that man is really himself; the invocation is his true being.

When this God-conscious invocation has become second nature for us, the question of knowing who we are or what we have been no longer arises: "All is well that ends well", the proverb says. We must become what we bear within ourselves from the Creator: our station before Him; and this in a certain sense was before the Creation. For since God is eternal, the consciousness of God may itself also be called eternal. Let this be your thought! All the rest is in God's hands.

4

There is indeed only "one thing needful", and it is impossible to avoid it within the framework of the human vocation, given on the one hand that our intelligence is made for the Truth and on the other hand that we have a soul to save.

To understand a religion in depth, one must understand religion as such: now the religious phenomenon is identified in its essence with the one and universal wisdom, hence with esoterism or the "primordial tradition", or if one prefers with the *philosophia perennis*. In other words esoteric wisdom is based doctrinally and methodically on what

135

is common to all religions or on what underlies each one of them. If I am repeating here something evident, it is to emphasize that one must never lose sight of this fact—for experience proves the temptation to do so is great—when engaged in the practice of an orthodox spirituality, that is, when one is surrounded by a framework of formalism or mythology.

There are three planes to consider in the human microcosm: namely, intelligence, will, and soul. The spiritual function of human intelligence—hence its essential function—is discernment between the Real and the illusory, the Absolute and the contingent, the Infinite and the finite, the Permanent and the impermanent; this is the one and universal Doctrine, hence the quintessence of all theology and all metaphysics. Then there is the will: the spiritual function of the human will, which is free, is essentially the concentration—in principle continuous—of the mind on the Real, the Absolute, the Infinite, the Permanent, or on the avataric Manifestation of the Real, which in practice amounts to the same; this is the Method, and it is the quintessence of all possible ways, for "prayer" is everything, and according to Saint Paul one must "pray without ceasing". Finally there is the soul, the character, sensibility, affectivity, the capacity to love: the spiritual function of the soul is essentially a quasi-existential conformation to the Real, namely virtue; this is Morality, not merely extrinsic and social, of course, but intrinsic and contemplative; without beauty of soul—I would even say without the sense of beauty—no spirituality is possible, displeasing as this may be for the ignorant and for pedants who imagine that with respect to metaphysical realization "technique" is all that matters, that is, a kind of coldly mechanical *yoga*. Discernment, concentration, virtue: it is these elements and nothing else that one must seek when engaged as a metaphysician in a traditional way; when practicing such a way, one must not be "converted" to a given theology or mythology, though one must love the symbols and their beauty in one's own religious cosmos as in that of others.

5

The immeasurable merit of Amida—or the merciful quality of the Absolute, in a more real or less unreal sense—can have the effect of instantaneously burning away the karmic layer of ignorance separating man from *Nirvâna*; it is not that *Nirvâna* is "given", but that ignorance is "removed".

Below this perspective, *Shinshû* declares the existence of a bhaktic Paradise located in the West, something that the simple faithful interpret literally.

In *Les Sectes bouddhiques japonaises* by Steinilber-Oberlin, one can read: "At the end of our earthly life, we cast off the last traces of this corrupted existence, and reborn in the Land of Purity and Happiness we obtain the Buddha's Enlightenment."

In the language of the *Tarîqah* we would say that the perfection of faith is the quintessence of the six themes of meditation and that it is this quintessence that creates the conditions for perfect receptivity with regard to the salvific and enlightening Grace contained in the divine Name, or more precisely in the Absolute this Name represents concretely. One could also say that what puts us definitively into contact with Grace is first pure Truth and second perfect Concentration; all of this coincides with "faith" as understood by Shinran.

Christian *gnosis* is directly analogous in a certain sense to *Shinshû* in that Redemption, hence the inexhaustible merit of Christ, is a manifestation—or the manifestation—of the merciful Power of the Infinite; Redemption does not "bestow" *gnosis*, but it removes what separates us from it if we know how to place ourselves into the requisite conditions. As in *Jôdo-Shinshû*, there is in Christianity a literal and bhaktic application and a metaphysical and jnanic application.

Shinshû is an ontological way, all things considered; what must be found—among a thousand possibilities—is the thread linking us to the Absolute; this thread appears to be infinitesimal, but it suffices because it is what it is.

6

According to some of the Greek Fathers and Orthodox theologians, the "Incarnation" brought about a kind of universal blessing, an effusion of "Christic" grace even outside the visible Church. In order to give this remarkable doctrine its full scope and complete universality, it is necessary to know that the "Incarnation" can touch non-Christians only on condition of being situated outside of history: the "Self" is "incarnated" in separativity or illusion; *Âtmâ* is "incarnated" in *Mâyâ*;

it is the entry into *Mâyâ*—giving rise to *Îshvara*—that constitutes the "Incarnation" *in divinis*, the eternal Incarnation; it is this Incarnation that has saved beings—first as possibilities—from nothingness, if one may put it this way. On a more reduced scale—or at a lesser degree of reality—the Incarnation is *Buddhi*, that is, the "sacrificial" entry of *Purusha* into Existence; it is the existential *fiat lux*, the illumination of darkness or chaos. In a more particular meaning, which concerns man, *Buddhi* saves in its capacity as Vishnu or Shiva, that is, through *bhakti* or *jnâna*; *Buddhi* has both an existential function and an intellectual function, and it is the second that can be termed "Christic". Christ manifests these prototypes of the "Incarnation" and "Redemption" historically and directly through his very person; but every other Revelation manifests them likewise, each in its fashion, depending on the aspects of the Real and possible perspectives.

Âtmâ, by entering *Mâyâ* as *Îshvara*, has "saved" possibilities from nothingness; *Îshvara* has saved potentialities from Non-Being and virtualities from non-manifestation; *Buddhi* saves beings—in an inverse and ascending manner—from negative manifestation, then manifestation as such; it does so objectively through the *Avatâra* and subjectively through the Intellect.

None of this in any way excludes the fact that the birth and death of Christ had the effect of bringing about a universal effusion of graces; but the same is true for each Revelation; in this case it is not a matter of decisive and salvific graces—which are already bestowed by the respective Revelation—but of vivifying graces; it is in this sense that the "Descent" (*tanzîl*) of the Koran can be said to mysteriously touch other spiritualities including the Christian or that the "Enlightenment" (*Bodhi*) of the Buddha illuminated Hindu spirituality. One can even say, paradoxically, that Christ vivified the esoterism of the Greco-Roman tradition even though it was perishing through the mere fact of his advent.

Some might object that Christ alone directly manifests the eternal "Incarnation" and that as a result the manner of manifesting it is indirect in the other Revelations; we would answer by saying that only the Buddha manifests the eternal *Bodhi* in a direct manner and that *Bodhi* appears therefore in an indirect manner in Christ, and so on and so forth. This is due to the fact that we speak of "Incarnation" because of Christ and of "Enlightenment" because of the Buddha; the possible designations of the prototype of Revelation and Deliverance are indefinite in number. There is in manifestation an unfolding of symbols, and each symbol refers to a real aspect of the divine Model or the universal models derived from it; but since it is a question here of the same principial and primordial reality, namely, the entry of the Absolute into relativity—whatever the degree considered—the modes or symbols are not mutually exclusive: the entry of the Koranic Revelation into the body of the Prophet can be termed an "incarnation" of the Word, just as the entry of the Holy Spirit—bearer of the Word—into the body of the Virgin is a "descent" of the divine Book; and likewise these two modes are within *Bodhi* as *Bodhi* is within them.

All of this is obvious to us, but I held to formulating it as I have just done. I intend to write on this subject. *In shâ'a 'Llâh.*

7

Space involves two essential Determinations: the Point and Extension or the Center and the Periphery; now inasmuch as the *Dhikr* is active or dynamic Perfection or the content, it corresponds analogically to the first element, and inasmuch as *Faqr* is passive or static Perfection or the container, it corresponds analogically to the second element.

Next, Space involves three Dimensions: Width, Height, and Depth or Length; and these can signify analogically *Makhâfah*, *Mahabbah*, and *Ma'rifah*.

Finally, one can distinguish six Directions in Space: North, South, East, West, Zenith, and Nadir; thus Abstention, Confidence, Accomplishment, Contentment, Discernment, and Union; or Void, Life, Act, Peace, Transcendence, Immanence.

In this way the whole Path is prefigured by Space and in Space.

8

Christianity is a bhaktic esoterism become religion; hence it is exoteric by its literalist and dogmatist interpretations and not by its symbolism or means, which are initiatic in their essence. Baptism and Confirmation taken together constitute Christian initiation; according to Guénon the sacraments later lost their initiatic character, but this is impossible in principle and in fact: in principle, because God never gives less than He promises—rather the opposite is true—and in fact, because it is technically impossible to bring about such a change, if only because of the dispersion of Christians starting from the first centuries. From the point of view of method, the central means is an ejaculatory orison containing the sacramental Name of Jesus or that of Mary, or both of them at once; the central *mantra* of Christianity—the support for concentration—is therefore *Jesu* or *Jesu Maria* in Latin or Greek. Whoever wishes to practice this method, which dates back to the origins of Christianity, must solemnly promise the Blessed Virgin to do so—in the form of a vow—in a sanctuary dedicated to her; he must also ask the Virgin's permission and implore her assistance, and this will have to be kept secret, at least *a priori* and under normal circumstances. And he will then have to renounce all the dispersing and degrading trivialities of the modern world; we must await death in a little spiritual garden and do so in the midst of our family life and worldly duties. God wants our soul and nothing else; if He demands something more from us, we shall know of this with certitude by giving Him our soul.

I write all this, Madame, out of duty so as not to overlook anything; therefore, I must tell you likewise that Islamic esoterism is also accessible in the West, but I have no reason *a priori* to go into further detail regarding it. That said, let us return to the essential. There are two moments in life, and these moments are everything: the present moment when we are free to choose what we want to be and the moment of death when we no longer have any choice and the decision belongs entirely to God. Now if the present moment is good, death will be good; if we are now with God—in this present that renews itself ceaselessly while remaining always the only actual moment—God will be with us at the moment of our death. The remembrance of God—ejaculatory orison—is a death in life; it will be a life in death.

Between the present moment when we remember God and the moment of death when God will remember us—and this reciprocity exists already in every prayer—there is the rest of life, the duration extending from the present moment until the last; but duration is but a succession of present moments, for we live always "now"; thus concretely and operatively speaking it is always the same blessed instant when we are free to remember God and to find our happiness in this remembrance.

P.S. Metaphysical truth and perpetual prayer, together with intrinsic virtue—virtue considered in terms of beauty—are the fundamental elements of the esoteric way and in the final analysis of all spirituality. And the divine Name contains in principle the totality of all sacramental means.

9

The Holy Name of Jesus contains all Truth and Grace; if one adds to it the Name of Mary, then one is placing special emphasis on the aspect of Grace, although this aspect is also contained in the Name of Jesus. It is advantageous to pronounce the Names in a liturgical or sacred language.

Even if all of our past has been nothing but error and disappointment, we must bless it if now, in this very instant, we have the grace of remembering God. Whoever stands before God or withdraws into Him has never lost anything. "The Kingdom of God is within you." And this Kingdom is now, not yesterday; it is here, not elsewhere: here in the sacred Name and in this blessed instant.

You tell me in your letter that your soul is often sad and discouraged; this is natural, but it is necessary above all not to allow bitterness to enter it, not even in a roundabout or indirect manner, for example by objectifying personal experiences. This would also be illogical since we know that others have had other experiences and that our experience is no more real than theirs.

Certainly your life is very agitated, but you must get into the habit of inserting in it the remembrance of God—the "act of love" as Sister Consolata would say—and this is possible in every circumstance.

The world is a battleground, and it is necessary that there be everywhere warriors of the Light, if I may express myself thus. In the meantime you are where Providence has placed you, and this means that there must be even there—in the chaos in which you live—someone who thinks of God or in other words who manifests the "remembrance". We must bear witness invisibly. In any case we have no choice; each must do as he is able.

Regarding confession, it must be considered in its strictly sacramental aspect. A person can always accuse himself for his infraction of rules, then for his lukewarmness, if he wishes, but it is not a question

141

of "personal secrets". The priest is the instrument of a sacramental grace and not necessarily a master; it is even very unlikely that he is a master, although he should be so and is so in principle.

Spiritual sincerity is a grace. One can always blame oneself for lacking in it, but this is in vain; God knows very well that a man is human. Therefore one must cling to God and have trust. The worst of errors is to close oneself to Mercy.

10

It is important not to underestimate—to say the least—the "moral" and "aesthetic" aspects of spirituality; what I mean by the first term are the virtues in the broadest sense of the word and by the second the forms and proportions of things, hence the symbolism of means of expression, for this symbolism is connected with the activity of the *barakah*.

While I am thinking of it: in my opinion one must avoid saying that the "supreme Principle" or the "Self" is superior to "God" or that metaphysics or "tradition" is more than "religion"—although tradition can be more, it is not necessarily so—or again that "initiation" is superior to "mysticism"; in other words one must not say that "God" is something "less", and this must not be said of "religion" or "mysticism" or the "saints" either. One must say—and this is more than a mere question of opportunity—that the "Self" is the "essence" or the "supreme reality" of God just as one must say, and as the disciples of Shaykh al-Alawi have assured me, that esoterism is the summit or quintessence of religion, and so on. In Arabic it would be completely ill sounding and even inconceivable to limit the Name *Allâh* in any fashion whatsoever or to separate *tasawwuf* from *dîn*; now Islam is a Semitic and monotheistic religion, like Christianity; what I do not accept for the one, I do not accept for the other. I know from experience that the Guénonian "believer" becomes intractable when he hears the words "God" and "religion", but this is unacceptable, especially when it is a question of the term "God"; I protest categorically, in the name of my function, against such a pernicious abuse of language. There are mysteries "in God"; there are none "beyond".

11

The first criterion of spirituality is that man demonstrate his consciousness of the incommensurability between the Real and the illusory, the Absolute and the relative, *Âtmâ* and *Mâyâ*, God and the world.

The second criterion is that man demonstrate his choice of the Real: that he understand the imperious necessity for active attachment to the Real, hence for a concrete, operative, and salvific relationship with God.

The third criterion is that man, knowing that the Real is the Sovereign Good and that it thus contains and projects all beauty, conform himself to it with all his soul; for what he knows to be perfect and what he wishes to attain, he must also be, and this he is through the virtues and not otherwise.

Man possesses an intelligence, a will, and a soul: a capacity for understanding, a capacity for willing, and a capacity for loving. Each of these three faculties contains an essential and supreme function, which is its reason for being and without which we would not be men, a function determined by the Real and contributing to salvation. Total knowledge, free will, and disinterested love; intelligence capable of absoluteness, will capable of sacrifice, soul capable of generosity.

All the dogmas, all the prescriptions, and all the means of a religion have their sufficient reason in the three fundamental vocations of man: in discernment, in practice, and in virtue. And all the gifts and means of a religion man bears within himself, but he no longer has access to them because of the fall: whence precisely the necessity—in principle relative—of outward forms, which awaken and actualize man's spiritual potentialities, but which also risk limiting them; whence in addition the necessity of esoterism.

The criterion of an authentic spirituality is not only consciousness of the primacy of *Âtmâ* and the relativity of *Mâyâ*, then the practice of a realizational and unitive method combined with the sincere practice of the virtues, but also—as a formal condition—a regular attachment to an intrinsically orthodox religion. It is only thus that a man presents himself as a "valid interlocutor" on the spiritual plane, first in relation to God and then in relation to his fellow men.

The spiritual life, we repeat, is first our consciousness of the nature of God, then our relationship with God, and finally the conditions for this relationship, both moral and traditional; for spirituality requires not only the conformation of our character to the divine Norm, but also extrinsically our integration into a sacred system.

There are two particularly pernicious pitfalls in the spiritual life: individualism and phenomenalism. The first consists in always considering oneself and in talking too readily about oneself; the second consists in always considering phenomena and in speaking of them improperly. All this is horizontal, not vertical; it is in accordance with *Mâyâ*, not in accordance with *Âtmâ*. One must never lose sight of our fundamental points of reference, the pillars of the Way. They must always shine through the manifestations of our immortal personality.

12

The past is indeed a matter of complete indifference, all the more as it is materially impossible in certain cases to verify to what degree we were right or wrong. It is not because we were right in the past that we are pleasing to God; it is because right now we give ourselves to Him in prayer and forget the past, whether good or bad.

And what matters is that God welcome us into Beatitude, not that He introduce us into some particular Paradise rather than another. "Deliverance" (*Moksha*) or the "Paradise of the Essence" (*Jannat al-Dhât*) is for the great sages; moreover every soul that is saved is in a certain manner "delivered". If we can hope to be saved—and we can by practicing prayer while abstaining from evil—the question of knowing where God will place us should be the least of our concerns.

Metaphysics is a boundless domain, and one must not wish to understand everything: first because not every man can understand everything and because one must be resigned to the possibility of having limitations, and second because the basic metaphysical truths are sufficient and because in prayer we possess all we need.

13

I see that S. persists in his anti-Platonism; were he right—and I wonder whether he is aware of this—all of Sufism and all the *Vedânta* would collapse along with Plato, given that the idea of relativity in principial Reality—*in divinis*, if one wishes—is essential to all metaphysics. Hence if the Platonists are mistaken, all the East is mistaken with them, including Buddhism, which also has the sense of relativity to the highest degree. S. believes that for the Platonists the idea of relativity in the Absolute—or the idea of a graduated Absolute—is true because it is logical, whereas in reality the relationship is the reverse: it is logical because it is true; no Platonist has ever said anything else. All things considered S. places before us the following dilemma: either to renounce Sufism, Vedantism, Buddhism and become Orthodox Christians, or else to reject Orthodoxy—or Christianity in general—as a heresy; for were he right in attributing this "sacred illogicality" to Christianity, we would have no other choice. What surprises me in all this is that he takes Christian theologians so earnestly when it should be easy to see what their human and intellectual limitations are by reading their books. Read the following in Gregory Palamas: "Pythagoras, Plato, and Socrates, in a manner low and unworthy of God, considered those models (the archetypes) as principles having their own existence. Hence they are the ones who should be accused of polytheism: indeed they had the heedlessness to introduce on their own initiative other divine natures, principles of beings, between the Supra-essential and creatures. . . . Divine wisdom tends essentially toward the following goal: to know what is the will of God, what is good, perfect, and pleasing to God." And there it is! The quoted text provides the key to the enigma: there is nothing relative *in divinis*— there is neither *Îshvara* nor *Purusha* nor *Prakriti*—because this would be "unworthy of God"! The sublime equals the absolute. And whosoever thinks otherwise is to be reviled.

14

An incident that appears to be a bad omen may not necessarily have this significance; it may signify either the exhaustion of a negative possibility, or an ambush of the devil seeking to trouble us in our thoughts or actions or to drive us into sadness, or again simply a paradox of *Mâyâ* having no other meaning than the play of contrasting possibilities. In this last case the ruse can be foiled by presence of mind and by way of a corrective stratagem: thus the Prophet, having fallen from his camel, said upon getting up, "Once in a lifetime God abases the one whom He has raised above everyone"; and thus Caesar, having taken a fall upon landing in Africa, said as he rose, "Scarcely am I in Africa, and I hold it between my two hands"—attitudes that have the quasi-magical virtue of neutralizing the caprice of *Mâyâ*, first within the soul and then with regard to others.

When the crown falls from the king's head at the moment of his coronation, this is assuredly a bad sign; but if it falls at some other moment, it may simply mean that God alone is King, and this reminder will be good for everyone.

In case of a bad sign—but this interpretation may itself be false—a man ought to say to himself: if this is the sign of something destined for me or something "written" (*maktûb*), hence something willed by God, I accept it in advance; for everything is ultimately for the good for a man who believes in God and who prays; the essential is to end up with God whatever the accidents along the path. This reflex produces in the soul resignation and serenity; and serenity is in harmony with devotion and the sense of the Sacred.

The contemplative who is penetrated by these qualities—which coincide with the love of God—will be able to proceed in an opposite sense: he will not come to serenity by way of resignation, but he will realize resignation by way of serenity; for nothing and no one can rob us of the supreme Good, unless we do so ourselves in our impatience and ingratitude. And where God is—in our Heart as in Heaven—there is Goodness, Beauty, Beatitude (*Rahmah*); whoever keeps himself close to this Treasure is at the Source of all he loves.

15

Allow me to mention some reflections on the analogy linking various orders with the symbolism of the elements; in comparing the ordinary state of the human spirit with a mound of earth, during a meditation in my dervish's cell, I was led to consider Liberation as having to be brought about by a passage through water, air, and fire before being fully realized in ether; and it seemed to me that everything without exception that can be said of the sensible elements and their reciprocal relationships also applies to these states of mind leading to Union. Moreover the symbolism can be transposed onto the mental plane in the sense that sentiment would correspond to earth, imagination to water, memory to air, reason to fire, the Intellect to ether. Through another transposition, the human body on the one hand and gross manifestation on the other correspond to earth, the human soul and subtle manifestation to water, the Intellect to air, Being to fire, and supreme Non-Being to ether. From another point of view, earth is humanity; water is the Church—or Tradition in general—or sacrifice or purification; air is the Son: the Word, the Prophet, the Doctrine; fire is the Holy Spirit, or Jibril or Revelation; ether is the Father, the Unique. Likewise "the Eternal Gospel" is ether; the four other Gospels are the other elements, the Gospel of Saint John, which is the last, being that of fire; and it is to be noted that Saint John is the author of the Apocalypse, which as a revelation is connected once again with the symbolism of fire.

There is something curious about Christianity in that it seems to have taken no account of the words of the crucified Christ to Saint John, making of him his bodily and spiritual brother; it seems to me there is a clear indication in this of the institution of something surpassing outward papacy; and in Islam Ali strikes me as sharing some analogy with Saint John. The fact that neither Saint John nor Ali has a permanent outward representative, whereas everyone accepts the papacy and the caliphate as something evident, results without doubt from the very nature of the principle of which these favorite disciples are the expressions. Just as water, represented above all by the seas, never leaves the earth, so the pope of the outward Church, who baptizes with water, never leaves humanity; fire on the contrary is not always on the earth, but dwells in the ether and comes out of it only periodically to manifest itself; likewise the pope of the inward Church, who baptizes with fire, is not always in the midst of humanity and manifests himself only in special circumstances. And again: the doctrinal infallibility of the pope, the descendant of Saint Peter, is outward and indirect, residing in the papal function itself; the infallibility of the descendant of Saint John, however, is inward and direct, residing in intellectual intuition. In the same way the papacy as a historical fact presents an outward continuity, which the function Christ bestowed upon Saint John does not require in order to be just as legitimate. Moreover the respective natures of both dignities manifest themselves clearly in the thunderstorm: rain falls without ceasing whereas lightning manifests itself periodically without any outward continuity. It could further be remarked that water cannot do without fire; if the igneous principle deserts it, it freezes and acquires thereby the outward properties of earth, namely, density and divisibility; and this applies also to the Church of Saint Peter, whose authority no longer rests on intellectual intuition, but simply on outward orthodoxy. And it is significant that it is Saint John who wrote these words: *In ipso vita erat, et vita erat lux hominum. Et lux in tenebris lucet, et tenebrae eam non comprehenderunt.*

16

The body is a tissue of sensations and instincts; the ego is a tissue of images and desires. All this is part of the current of forms, which is not our true Self. The supreme Name is the expression and receptacle of our true Self; it is not really part of the current of forms; in it we are perfectly ourselves. It is the "form of the Non-formal"—or "the Supra-formal"—and the "manifestation of the Non-manifest". Shankara says: "Distinguish between the ephemeral and the Real, repeat the Holy Name of God, and thus calm the agitated mind."

The man who has been seized by the supreme Name, he in whom the Name has firmly established itself to the point of becoming second nature, possesses a mind so different from that of the ordinary man— the man still imprisoned in the tumult of this lower world—that a sudden transition from the profane to the sanctified mind would amount to a mortal rupture. The outer rotation of a wheel must be compared with its inner rotation, which takes place near the hub: it is the same wheel, the same movement, but the inner rotation is center and cause, whereas the outer rotation is circumference and effect. And since there can be no sudden transition from one degree of reality to another—except by a grace man is unable to command—it is of the utmost importance that he should place his life, his thoughts, and his wishes within the framework of the Tradition; thus many shocks will be neutralized in advance, many oppositions will be smoothed out, and many hardnesses will be gradually dissolved.

"I sleep, but my heart waketh": the ego sleeps, absorbed by the Name; but the Self, made present by the Name, is in the state of eternal waking. The Self radiates through the eyes that sleep.

The ego affirms itself most noisily where the movement of the wheel is quickest: just as agitated water is scattered into innumerable drops, so the Self is as if segmented at the edge of the cosmic wheel into innumerable souls. The current of forms—which is illusory—is at once movement and division; where the rotation is, there the scattering of egos takes place, the ego being a consequence of the universal rotation. Where all is calm, there the Self is, eternal and indivisible; where the center is, there is Oneness. And since the cosmic wheel is none other than the Self, there is no point at which the Self may not rise up like a saving miracle.

EDITOR'S NOTES

Numbers in bold indicate pages in the text for which the following citations and explanations are provided.

The Sense of the Absolute in Religions

4: "And the *Word* was *made flesh*, and dwelt among us" (John 1:14).

The mystery of Sinai: "When the children of Israel were gone forth out of the land of Egypt, the same day came they into the wilderness of Sinai. . . . And Moses went up unto God, and the Lord called unto him out of the mountain, saying, Thus shalt thou say to the house of Jacob, and tell the children of Israel: Ye have seen what I did unto the Egyptians, and how I bare you on eagles' wings, and brought you unto myself. Now therefore, if ye will obey my voice indeed, and keep my covenant, then ye shall be a peculiar treasure unto me above all people: for all the earth is mine. And ye shall be unto me a kingdom of priests, and an holy nation" (Exod. 19:1-6).

5: "*Closer than your jugular vein*": "We verily created a man and We know what his soul whispereth to him, and We are nearer to him than his jugular vein" (*Sûrah "Qâf"* [50]:16).

6: Note 3: "Jesus said unto them, Verily, verily, I say unto you, *Before Abraham was, I am*" (John 8:58).

7: In the author's original French, the term rendered "evidence" in the phrase *metaphysical evidence* is *évidence*, which includes the idea of obviousness or self-evidence, while at the same time suggesting corroboration or proof.

Note 3 (cont.): The French Islamicist Louis *Massignon* (1883-1962), best known for his magisterial study of the Sufi saint Mansur al-Hallaj, published an article entitled "Christ in the Gospels according to al-Ghazzali" in 1932.

Abu Hatim al-Razi (874-934) was a prominent Ismaili philosopher and theologian.

8: "*The soul is all that it knows*": According to *Aristotle* (384-322 B.C.), "The thinking part of the soul, while impassible, must be capable of receiving the form of an object; that is, it must be potentially identical in character with its object without being the object" (*On the Soul*, 3.4).

9: "Jesus saith unto him, *I am the way, the truth, and the life*: no man cometh unto the Father, but by me" (John 14:6).

10: Note 4: *Cabalists* are Jewish mystics and esoterists.

11: Note 5: *Myth of Indra*: Ananda K. Coomaraswamy (see editor's note for "Vicissitudes of Spiritual Temperaments", p. 34, Note 2) writes, "If we consider the miraculous life [of the Buddha], we shall find that almost every detail, from the free choice of the time and place of birth to the lateral birth itself and the taking of the Seven Strides, and from the Going Forth to the Great Awakening on the strewn altar at the foot of the World-tree at the Navel of the Earth, and from the defeat of the Dragons to the miraculous kindling of the sacrificial firewood, can be exactly paralleled . . . in the Vedic mythology of Agni and Indra, priest and king *in divinis*" (*Hinduism and Buddhism*, Part II, "The Doctrine"). In the most famous of his epic exploits, the god Indra enters into battle against the serpent-demon Vritra—in Sanskrit, a "storm-cloud" of ignorance and sloth—who holds the rivers of the world in his coils, preventing them from flowing for the benefit of man; when this "Dragon" is destroyed, the benefic waters are released along with the sun and the dawns.

Note 6: Charles *Péguy* (1873-1914) was a French thinker and poet who sought to combine certain Christian ideas with a Utopian brand of socialism.

12: The *Golden Legend*, a medieval manual compiled by Jacob of Voragine (c. 1230-c. 1298) and organized in accordance with the liturgical year, consists of the lives of the saints and short meditations on the major Christian festivals.

Note 8: "*Three Mary Magdalenes*": Roman Catholic tradition associates Mary Magdalene with three distinct figures mentioned in the Scriptures: "a woman in the city, which was a sinner", who washed Jesus' feet "with tears, and did wipe them with the hairs of her head, and kissed his feet, and anointed them with ointment" (Luke 7:37-38); "Mary called Magdalene, out of whom went seven devils" (Luke 8:2); and the sister of Lazarus and Martha, who "sat at Jesus' feet, and heard his word", whom Christ commended, saying, "One thing is needful: and Mary hath chosen that good part, which shall not be taken away from her" (Luke 10:39, 42; cf. John 11:1-2).

14: Note 11: *Valmiki* is the traditional author of the *Râmâyana*, the epic story of the *avatâra Rama*; when pronounced backwards, "Rama" becomes "Mara", the name of a diabolical spirit of pestilence and mortal disease.

15: *The "faith that moves mountains"*: "If ye have faith as a grain of mustard seed, ye shall say unto this mountain, Remove hence to yonder place; and it shall remove; and nothing shall be impossible unto you" (Matt. 17:20).

16: Note 13: *Prologue to the Gospel of John*: John 1:1-18.

The talk by night with Nicodemus: "There was a man of the Pharisees, named Nicodemus, a ruler of the Jews; the same came to Jesus by night" (John 3:1-2).

"In my Father's house are many mansions: if it were not so, I would have told you. I go to prepare a place for you" (John 14:2).

Is There a Natural Mysticism?

23: The phrase "natural mysticism" is used in the title and throughout this chapter to translate *mystique naturelle*, despite the sometimes equivocal meaning of the word "mysticism" in English; for the author "mysticism" always denotes a genuine, supra-rational insight into spiritual Truth.

27: *Shankarian Vedantism* is the non-dual doctrine of Shankara (788-820), one of the most influential sages in the history of India, whom the author regarded as the greatest of Hindu metaphysicians.

Vishnuism, or Vaishnavism, is a theistic sect of the Hindu religion whose members worship the God Vishnu as the Supreme Deity.

Amidism is the Buddhist *Jôdo* or Pure Land sect, whose central spiritual practice is the invocation of Amida, the Buddha of "infinite light".

"The wind *bloweth where it listeth*, and thou hearest the sound thereof, but canst not tell whence it cometh, and whither it goeth: so is every one that is born of the Spirit" (John 3:8).

28: Note 4: *Bernard* of Clairvaux (1090-1153) was a Cistercian monk and the author of numerous homilies on the Song of Songs.

The *Sukhâvatî-Vyûha*s are Buddhist Scriptures of the *Jôdo* or Pure Land school that describe in great detail the paradisiacal world of *Sukhâvatî* ("place of bliss"), into which will be born all those who invoke Amida with faith.

29: *Amitabha* (Sanskrit) or Amida (Japanese) is the name of the Buddha of "infinite light", who as a *bodhisattva* named Dharmakara vowed not to enter *Nirvâna* until he had brought all who invoked his Name into the paradise of his Pure Land, also known as *Sukhâvatî* ("place of bliss") or the Western Paradise.

Note 5: *Hesychasm*, practiced by those whose aim is to attain a state of *hesychia* or inner stillness through practice of the Jesus Prayer or other "prayer of the heart", is the predominant form of spirituality in the Christian East.

30: *Honen Shonin* (1133-1212), founder of the *Jôdo* or Pure Land school of Japanese Buddhism, taught that everyone without exception can be reborn into the "pure land" promised by the Buddha Amida simply by faithful repetition of Amida's Name.

Teresa of Avila (1515-82), a Spanish Carmelite nun and mystic, wrote extensively on the stages of the spiritual life and the levels of prayer.

Vicissitudes of Spiritual Temperaments

34: "The wind *bloweth where it listeth*, and thou hearest the sound thereof, but canst not tell *whence it cometh, and whither it goeth*: so is every one that is born of the Spirit" (John 3:8).

Note 2: *Ananda Coomaraswamy* (1877-1947), curator of Indian art in the Boston Museum of Fine Arts and one of the founding figures of the traditionalist or perennialist school, was the author of numerous books and articles on art, religion, and metaphysics.

According to a French tradition, *Mary Magdalene*, who was among the women followers of Christ and one of the first witnesses of his resurrection, journeyed with her brother Lazarus to Marseilles, where she assisted in converting the whole of Provence before entering into a life of seclusion for the remaining thirty years of her life.

The anchorite Paul (c. 230-342), also known as Paul of Thebes and traditionally regarded as the first Christian hermit, was among the earliest of the Desert Fathers of Egypt (see editor's note for this chapter, p. 35, Note 3), where he lived in a cave for nearly one hundred years.

Mary of Egypt (c. 344-c. 421), formerly an actress and courtesan, found herself barred from crossing the threshold of the Holy Sepulcher in Jerusalem; instructed by a voice from Heaven to flee to the desert to repent of her sins, she spent the next forty-seven years in complete solitude, receiving the Eucharist from the priest Zosimus only once at the end of her life.

35: For *Teresa of Avila*, see editor's note for "Is There a Natural Mysticism?", p. 30.

Note 3: The *Desert Fathers* were Christian ascetics and hermits of the third, fourth, and fifth centuries who withdrew to the wilderness in Egypt, Syria, Palestine, and Arabia to lead lives of contemplative prayer.

37: Canonized as *Teresa of the Child Jesus*, Thérèse of Lisieux (1873-97), popularly known as "The Little Flower" and distinctive for the emphasis she placed on the importance of remaining "small" before God, was a Carmelite nun who had been drawn to the life of prayer as a very young child.

39: *The familiar Gospel teaching*: "Verily I say unto you, Inasmuch as ye have done it unto one of the least of these my brethren, ye have done it unto me" (Matt. 25:40).

Note 7: *Ramakrishna* (1834-86), a devotee of the goddess Kali, was one of the greatest Hindu saints of modern times, notable for his ability to adapt to the needs of many kinds of disciples depending on whether they envisaged God, as he said, "with form" or "without form".

40: *"Sin against the Holy Spirit"*: "All manner of sin and blasphemy shall be forgiven unto men: but the blasphemy against the Holy Spirit shall not be forgiven unto men" (Matt. 12:31; cf. Luke 12:10). Elsewhere the author writes: "Sins against the Holy Spirit exclude those dispositions of soul through which the remission of sins takes place. They are six in number: (1) Presumption (overestimating oneself, in principle or in fact); (2) Despair (doubting God's Mercy); (3) Attack against the known truth; (4) Envy of another's gifts of grace; (5) Obstinacy (in evil, intellectual or moral); (6) Final Impenitence (in the face of death)" (see *The Fullness of God: Frithjof Schuon on Christianity*, ed. James S. Cutsinger [Bloomington, Indiana: World Wisdom, 2004], p. 169).

41: "Behold, I send you forth as sheep in the midst of wolves: be ye therefore *wise as serpents*, and *harmless as doves*" (Matt. 10:16).

"There are diversities of gifts, but the same Spirit. . . . For to one is given by the Spirit the word of wisdom . . . to another *discerning of spirits*" (1 Cor. 12:4, 8, 10).

42: Note 12: Mohandas K. *Gandhi* (1869-1948) was well known for spinning the cotton for his clothing on a handloom and for advocating a return to the simplicity of village craftsmanship.

43: "Woe unto the world because of offences! *for it must needs be that offences come*; but woe to that man by whom the offence cometh!" (Matt. 18:7).

"Thou carriest them away as with a flood; they are as a sleep: in the morning they are *like grass which groweth up*. In the morning it flourisheth, and groweth up; *in the evening it is cut down, and withereth*" (Ps. 90 [A Prayer of Moses the Man of God]:5-6).

"*Seek ye first the kingdom of God, and His righteousness; and all these things shall be added unto you*" (Matt. 6:33; cf. Luke 12:31).

44: Note 13: For *Shankara*, see editor's note for "Is There a Natural Mysticism?", p. 27.

Soren *Kierkegaard* (1813-55) was a Danish existentialist of whom the author has written: "Why was Kierkegaard neither Platonist nor Aristotelian nor Scholastic nor Palamite? Is it because he was a Vedantist or Mahayanist? Certainly not. Consequence: his doctrine is null and void. The proof of this is that he rejects 'organized' Christianity, hence the traditional theology that upholds it, and he does so in favor of a subjectivism that is not intellectual (for in that case he would have acknowledged objective metaphysics, whose mode of expression perforce is rational and abstract) but voluntaristic and sentimental, whence comes his subjectivistic or individualistic moralism, his insistence on thinking 'existentially', his nullity from the point of view of the real and efficacious spirituality that saves" ("Letter on Existentialism", *The Essential Frithjof Schuon*, ed. Seyyed Hossein Nasr [Bloomington, Indiana: World Wisdom, 2005], p. 492).

Johann Wolfgang von *Goethe* (1749-1832) was a German poet, novelist, and playwright, of whom the author has said: "[Goethe] was the victim of his epoch owing to the fact that humanism in general and Kantianism in particular had vitiated his tendency toward a vast and finely shaded wisdom; he thus became, quite paradoxically, the spokesman of a perfectly bourgeois 'horizontality'" (*To Have a Center* [Bloomington, Indiana: World Wisdom Books, 1990], p. 16).

Yogananda (1893-1952), founder in 1925 of the "Self-Realization Fellowship", advocated a form of "yoga" based on "practical efforts" and universal love, which he claimed had been lost in the "dark ages" of India and rediscovered by his own lineage of teachers only in "modern times".

45: Note 13 (cont.): *Homage to Ananda K. Coomaraswamy: A Memorial Volume: A Garland of Tributes*, edited by S. Durai Raja Singam, was published in 1952.

46: *None come to the "Father" except by the "Son"*: "I am the way, the truth, and the life: no man cometh unto the Father, but by me" (John 14:6).

Note 14: For *Hesychasm*, see editor's note for "Is There a Natural Mysticism?", p. 29, Note 5.

The "*Jesus Prayer*", which is the most common invocatory prayer in the Eastern Christian tradition, consists of the words—or some variation—"Lord Jesus Christ, Son of God, have mercy upon us."

Note 15: For *Amidism*, see editor's note for "Is There a Natural Mysticism", p. 27.

For *Honen*, see editor's note for "Is There a Natural Mysticism", p. 30.

Shinran (1173-1262), a disciple of Honen and founder of the *Jôdo-Shinshû* or "true pure land school" of Japanese Buddhism, rejected all "ways of effort" and advocated complete reliance on the "power of the other" as manifest in the Name of the Buddha Amida, a single pronunciation of which is sufficient for rebirth in the Buddha's paradise, *Sukhâvatî*.

47: *He has "harmlessness" without having* . . . *"wisdom"*: "Behold, I send you forth as sheep in the midst of wolves: be ye therefore wise as serpents, and harmless as doves" (Matt. 10:16).

Note 16: "And the *light* shineth in darkness; and the *darkness* comprehended it not" (John 1:5).

49: Note 18: *Guillaume de Saint-Amour* (c. 1200-1272) was author of a short treatise "On the Dangers of the Present Time", in which he attacked the new religious orders of the thirteenth century, including the Dominicans, on the grounds that they were too concerned with worldly matters, an attack that prompted a strong defense of the orders by Thomas Aquinas, himself a Dominican friar.

Thomas Aquinas (c. 1225-74), a giant among the medieval scholastics and a doctor of the Catholic Church, taught that "*an error concerning the creation, by subjecting it to causes other than God, engenders a false science of God*, and takes men's minds away from Him, to whom faith seeks to lead them" (*Summa contra Gentiles*, Bk. 2, Ch. 3, Sect. 6).

Pierre *Teilhard de Chardin* (1881-1955), a French Jesuit paleontologist and heterodox theological writer, claimed that traditional Christian theology, especially its teachings concerning the creation and fall of man, had been rendered outmoded by modern evolutionary biology and that Christ should be reconceived as the "Omega Point", the culmination of a universal development beginning with matter.

The Doctrine of Illusion

53: Note 1: For *Ramakrishna*, see editor's note for "Vicissitudes of Spiritual Temperaments", p. 39, Note 7.

54: Note 3: *Gaudapada* (sixth or seventh century A.D.)—the teacher of Govindapada, who in turn was the teacher of Shankara—was the author of a *kârikâ*, or commentary, on the *Mândûkya Upanishad*, in which he was one of the first to set forth the basic principles of *Advaita Vedânta*.

For *Shankaracharya* (that is, Shankara), see editor's note for "Is There a Natural Mysticism?", p. 27.

56: Note 7: Arthur *Schopenhauer* (1788-1860), a German Kantian philosopher, is well known for observing that solipsism "needs not so much a refutation as a cure".

57: Note 8: The author's *Perspectives spirituelles et faits humains* was first published in French in 1953 (Paris: Cahiers du Sud) and in a second edition in 1989 (Paris: Maisonneuve and Larose); it appeared in an English translation as *Spiritual Perspectives and Human Facts* in 1953 (London: Faber and Faber, trans. MacLeod Matheson) and again in 1970 (London: Perennial Books, trans. P. N. Townsend).

Gnosis: Language of the Self

61: Note 1: According to *Clement of Alexandria* (c. 150-c. 215), head of the famous Christian Catechetical School of ancient Alexandria, "the gnostic alone is truly devout", for spiritual perfection consists precisely in being "assimilated to God" through knowledge (*gnosis*) of the divine nature, this being "the most important of all things" (*Stromateis*, Book 7).

Jakob *Boehme* (1575-1624), a German mystic and esoterist, used the term "theosophist" in its etymological sense to refer to someone who has mastered the deep "wisdom" (*sophia*) of "God" (*theos*); see such works of Boehme's as *On the Election of Grace and Theosophical Questions* and *Six Theosophical Points*.

Note 2: *Sapiential doctrines*: The author writes elsewhere, "The demiurgic tendency is conceived in the *Vedânta* as an objectification, and in Sufism it is conceived as an individuation and so in fact as a subjectification, God being then not pure 'Subject' as in the Hindu perspective, but pure 'Object', 'He' (*Huwa*), That which no subjective vision limits. This divergence lies only in the form, for it goes without saying that the 'Subject' of the *Vedânta* is anything but an individual determination and that the Sufic 'Object' is anything but the effect of an 'ignorance'. The 'Self' (*Âtmâ*) is 'He', for it is 'purely objective' inasmuch as it excludes all individuation, and the 'He' (*Huwa*) is 'Self' and so 'purely subjective' in the sense that it excludes all objectification" (*Spiritual Perspectives and Human Facts*, trans. P. N. Townsend [London: Perennial Books, 1970], Part 4, "The *Vedânta*", p. 102).

62: Note 3: "*I am the light of the world*; he that followeth me shall not walk in darkness, but shall have the light of life" (John 8:12).

"I am the way, the truth, and the life: *no man cometh unto the Father, but by me*" (John 14:6).

Note 4: *Meister Eckhart* (c. 1260-1327), a German Dominican writer who was regarded by the author as the greatest of Christian metaphysicians and esoterists, defined the Intellect *in an ambiguous manner* in saying that "there is something in the soul that is uncreated and uncreatable, and this is the Intellect".

63: "*Come down from Heaven*": "I believe . . . in one Lord Jesus Christ, the only-begotten Son of God . . . who for us men and for our salvation came down from heaven, and was incarnate of the Holy Spirit and the Virgin Mary, and was made man" (Nicene Creed; cf. John 3:13).

64: Note 8 (cont.): "Give not *that which is holy* unto the *dogs*, neither *cast* ye your *pearls before swine*, lest they trample them under their feet, and turn again and rend you" (Matt. 7:6).

65: "*God alone is God*": "He is God, the One! God, the eternally besought of all! He begetteth not nor was begotten. And there is none comparable unto Him" (*Sûrah* "The Unity" [112]:1-4); *passim*.

Eckhartian texts are the writings of Meister Eckhart (see editor's note above).

Note 9: Mansur *al-Hallaj* (858-922), the first Sufi martyr, was flayed and crucified by the exoteric authorities for his mystical pronouncement, *Anâ 'l-Haqq*, "I am the Truth."

Bayazid (Abu Yazid) al-Bastami (d. 874), known as the "sultan of the gnostics", is said to have been the first of the great Sufi masters to teach the doctrine of *fanâ'* or spiritual extinction in God.

"*He who has seen me has seen the Truth (God)*" and the other sayings cited by the author in this note are *ahâdîth* of the Prophet Muhammad.

66: "*Wisdom according to the flesh*": "In simplicity and godly sincerity, not with fleshly wisdom, but by the grace of God, we have had our conversation in the world" (2 Cor. 1:12).

67: "For whosoever will save his life shall lose it: and whosoever will *lose his life* for my sake shall find it" (Matt. 16:25); "He that loveth his life shall lose it; and he that hateth his life in this world shall *keep it* unto life eternal" (John 12:25); *passim*.

"Behold, *the kingdom of God is within you*" (Luke 17:21).

Note 11 (cont.): "*There is no lustral water like unto knowledge*" is a traditional Hindu teaching often quoted by the author, based in one of its formulations on the *Bhagavad Gîtâ*, 4:38.

The *Law of Manu* is an ancient collection of moral, social, and legal prescriptions understood to be binding on all orthodox Hindus.

Note 12: "*And the light shineth in darkness; and the darkness comprehended it not*" (John 1:5).

"*Inasmuch as ye have done it unto one of the least of these my brethren, ye have done it unto me*" (Matt. 25:40).

For Ananda K. *Coomaraswamy*, see editor's note for "Vicissitudes of Spiritual Temperaments", p. 34, Note 2.

For *Shankara*, see editor's note for "Is There a Natural Mysticism?", p. 27.

67-68: "Jesus answered, Verily, verily, I say unto thee, Except a man be born of water and of the Spirit, he cannot enter into the kingdom of God. That which is born of the flesh is flesh; and *that which is born of the Spirit is spirit*. Marvel not that I said unto thee, Ye must be born again. The wind bloweth where it listeth, and thou hearest the sound thereof, but *canst not tell whence it cometh, and whither it goeth*: so is every one that is *born of the Spirit*" (John 3:5-8).

68: "*No man hath ascended up to heaven, but he that came down from heaven, even the Son of man which is in heaven*" (John 3:13).

Plato (427-347 B.C.), greatest of the ancient Greek philosophers and the pupil of *Socrates* (c. 470-399 B.C.), writes of his master's final teaching in the dialogue *Phaedo*: "Those who really apply themselves in the right way to philosophy are directly and of their own accord preparing themselves for dying and death" (64a); for death is "nothing more or less than this, the separate condition of the body by itself when it is released from the soul and the separate condition by itself of the soul when released from the body" (64c).

"In the beginning was the Word, and the Word was with God, and the Word was God. . . . *All things were made* by him; and without him *was not any thing made that was made*" (John 1:1, 3).

Note 13 (cont.): *René Guénon* (1886-1951), a French metaphysician, prolific scholar of religions, and one of the formative authorities of the traditionalist or perennialist school, published *Man and His Becoming according to the Vedânta* in 1925.

Note 14: Daisetz Teitaro *Suzuki* (1870-1966) included an article on "The *Kôan* Exercise and the *Nembutsu*" (Essay I, Pt. II, Ch. 1) in his second series of *Essays in Zen Buddhism*, published in 1933.

Note 15: *Gregory of Nazianzus* (329-89), also known as Gregory the Theologian, was one of the most important Fathers of the Eastern Church and the author of five "Theological *Discourses*", or "Orations", containing most notably a detailed treatment of the doctrine of the Holy Spirit.

69: "And the *Word* was *made flesh*" (John 1:14).

70: "*The world is false;* Brahma *is true*; the soul is not other than *Brahma*": this summation of *Advaita Vedânta* is traditionally ascribed to Shankara.

"An invisible and subtle essence is the Spirit that pervades the whole universe. That is Reality. That is Truth. *That art Thou*" (*Chândogya Upanishad*, 6.14.3).

"The *yogin* whose intellect is perfect contemplates all things as abiding in himself, and thus by the eye of knowledge he perceives that *everything is Âtmâ*" (*Chândogya Upanishad*, 6.1.4).

"The Self was indeed *Brahma* in the beginning. It knew only that '*I am Brahma*'. Therefore It became all. And whoever among the gods knew It also became That; and the same with sages and men. . . . And to this day whoever in like manner knows '*I am Brahma*' becomes all this universe. Even the gods cannot prevail against him, for he becomes their Self" (*Brihadâranyaka Upanishad*, 1.4.10).

71: "*All that is to be found on earth is cursed save the remembrance of God*" and "*There is no fault greater than that of existence*" are *ahâdîth* of the Prophet Muhammad.

"Why callest thou me good? *There is none good but one, that is, God*" (Matt. 19:17, Mark 10:18; cf. Luke 18:19).

72: Note 17: Angelus *Silesius*, that is, the "Silesian Angel", was the penname of Johannes Scheffler (1624-77), a Roman Catholic priest and mystical poet greatly influenced by the teachings of Meister Eckhart.

Omar Khayyam (1048-1125) was a Persian astronomer, mathematician, and poet, best known for his mystical *Rubaiyat* ("quatrains").

74: According to Hindu tradition, the sacred waters of the lake *Mani-karnika*, which lies in close proximity to the river Ganges in the city of

Benares, are the perspiration that flowed from Vishnu when he finished creating the world.

The Ternary Aspect of the Human Microcosm

77: Note 2: *The law of "inverse analogy"*: René *Guénon* (see editor's note for "*Gnosis*: Language of the Self", p. 68, Note 13) quotes the following passage from the *Upanishads*, "This *Âtmâ*, which dwells in the heart, is smaller than a grain of rice, smaller than a grain of barley, smaller than a grain of mustard, smaller than a grain of millet, smaller than the germ which is in the grain of millet; this *Âtmâ*, which dwells in the heart, is also greater than the earth (the sphere of gross manifestation), greater than the atmosphere (the sphere of formless manifestation), greater than all the world together (that is, beyond all manifestation, being the unconditioned)" (*Chândogya Upanishad*, 3.14.3); then Guénon comments: "This is so, in fact, because analogy is necessarily applied in an inverse sense . . . and just as the image of an object is inverted relatively to that object, that which is first or greatest in the principial order is, apparently at any rate, last and smallest in the order of manifestation" (*Man and His Becoming according to the Vedânta*, Ch. 3, "The Vital Center of the Human Being, Seat of *Brahma*").

78: "The *yogin* whose intellect is perfect contemplates all things as abiding in himself, and thus by the eye of knowledge he perceives that *everything is Âtmâ*" (*Chândogya Upanishad*, 6.1.4).

Note 6: The *Eckhartian distinction* is that of Meister Eckhart (see editor's note for "*Gnosis*: Language of the Self", p. 62, Note 4), who taught that "the Intellect, which looks inside and surveys all the recesses of the *Godhead* . . . penetrates within. It is not satisfied with goodness or with wisdom or with truth or with *God* Himself. In good truth, it is as little satisfied with God as with a stone or a tree. It never rests; it bursts into the ground from which goodness and truth come forth and perceives God's being *in principio*, in the beginning, where goodness and truth are going out, before it acquires any name, before it bursts forth" (*Sermon* 69).

79: Note 8: "In the creation of the heavens and the earth and (in) the difference of night and day are tokens (of His sovereignty) for men of understanding, such as remember God, standing, sitting, and reclining" (*Sûrah* "The Family of Imran" [3]:190-91); "When ye have performed the act of worship, remember God, standing, sitting, and reclining" (*Sûrah* "Women" [4]:103).

80: "*I sleep, but my heart waketh*" (Song of Sol. 5:2).

"And *the Word* was *made flesh*, and dwelt among us" (John 1:14).

Love of God, Consciousness of the Real

81: Note 1: For *René Guénon* and *L'Homme et son devenir selon le Vedânta*, see editor's note for "*Gnosis*: Language of the Self", p. 68, Note 13.

83: "Think not that I am come to *destroy* the law, or the prophets: I am not come to destroy, but to *fulfill*" (Matt. 5:17).

Note 3: "And thou shalt love the Lord thy God with all thine heart, and with all thy soul, and with all thy might" (Deut. 6:5); "And now, Israel, what doth the Lord thy God require of thee, but to fear the Lord thy God, to walk in all His ways, and to love Him, and to serve the Lord thy God with all thy heart and with all thy soul" (Deut. 10:12); "Jesus said unto him, Thou shalt love the Lord thy God with all thy heart, and with all thy soul, and with all thy mind" (Matt. 22:37); "And thou shalt love the Lord thy God with all thy heart, and with all thy soul, and with all thy mind, and with all thy strength: this is the first commandment" (Mark 12:30); "And he answering said, Thou shalt love the Lord thy God with all thy heart, and with all thy soul, and with all thy strength, and with all thy mind; and thy neighbor as thyself" (Luke 10:27).

84: Note 5: For *Bernard* of Clairvaux, see editor's note for "Is There a Natural Mysticism", p. 28, Note 4.

Francis of Assisi (c. 1181-1226), founder of the Order of Friars Minor, is well known for his love of the beauty of nature, as expressed in his "Canticle of the Sun", a hymn in praise of the radiation of the Divine in creation.

Fra Angelico (1387-1455) was a Dominican friar of the monastery of Fiesole, Italy, as well as a famous painter of the Florentine School.

The *Fedeli d'Amore* ("liegemen of love") were a group of medieval poets, including Dante, who transposed the courtly ideal of love for the earthly beloved—in Dante's case, Beatrice—into a means of deepening one's love for God.

85: "*God alone is good*": "Why callest thou me good? There is none good but one, that is, God" (Matt. 19:17, Mark 10:18, Luke 18:19).

Seeing God Everywhere

88: Note 2: For *Meister Eckhart*, see editor's note for "*Gnosis*: Language of the Self", p. 62, Note 4.

89: "And Our word unto a thing, when We intend it, is only that We say unto it: *Be!* and it is" (*Sûrah* "The Bee" [16]:40).

100: "Enter ye in at the strait gate: for wide is the gate, and broad is the way, that leadeth to destruction, and many there be which go in thereat: Because *strait is the gate*, and narrow is the way, which leadeth unto life, and few there be that find it" (Matt. 7:13-14).

"Verily I say unto you, That *a rich man shall hardly enter into the kingdom of heaven*" (Matt. 19:23).

Some Observations

103: "I am the *Light of the world*" (John 9:5).

Origen (c. 185-c. 254), together with several other early Church Fathers, speaks of Christ as the *Wisdom of the Father*.

"And *the Light shineth in darkness*; and the darkness comprehended it not" (John 1:5).

104: In reciting the Nicene Creed, Orthodox Christians confess that the Holy Spirit *"proceeds from the Father"* alone *in divinis*, though the Spirit was *"delegated by the Son"* in time (cf. John 15:26); but in the Roman Catholic Church the term *Filioque* is added to the Latin text of the Creed, signifying that the Spirit proceeds from the Father "and the Son".

Note 3: The *Decalogue* consists of the "Ten Commandments" given by God to Moses (cf. Ex. 20:3-17); in the Cabala, or Jewish mystical tradition, the *Sephiroth* (literally "numbers" in Hebrew) are the ten emanations of *Ein Sof*, the Supreme Godhead.

105: λειτουργία (*leitourgia*), or "liturgy", is etymologically the "work" (*ergon*) of the "people" (*laos*).

On *Calvary* Christ addresses his Mother in reference to John: "Woman, behold thy *son*!" (John 19:26).

"*Feed my sheep*" (John 21:16, 17).

Note 4: *Augustine* (354-430) was *Bishop* of the North African city of *Hippo* and the greatest of the Western Church Fathers.

105-106: At the sea of *Tiberias* Christ says of John that he will "tarry *till I come*" (John 21:22).

"Thou art Peter, and upon this rock I will build my church; and *the gates of hell shall not prevail against it*" (Matt. 16:18).

106: The three "*Evangelical counsels*" of poverty, chastity, and obedience, also known as the "counsels of perfection", gave rise to the traditional vows of the monk.

Note 7: Quintus Septimius Florens *Tertullian* (c. 160-c. 225) was an early Christian apologist and ascetical writer, whose works include a short treatise "On Baptism".

Dionysius the Areopagite (dated c. 500 by many scholars), a disciple of Saint Paul's (cf. Acts 17:34) and the author of several important mystical works, writes of the sacraments in his *Ecclesiastical Hierarchy*.

107: *The miracle of the bread*: "And he commanded the multitude to sit down on the grass, and took the five loaves, and the two fishes, and looking up to heaven, he blessed, and brake, and gave the loaves to his disciples, and the disciples to the multitude. And they did all eat, and were filled: and they took up of the fragments that remained twelve baskets full" (Matt. 14:19-20; cf. Mark 6:38-44, Luke 9:13-17).

The miracle of the wine: "Jesus saith unto them, Fill the waterpots with water. And they filled them up to the brim. And he saith unto them, Draw out now, and bear unto the governor of the feast. And they bare it. When the ruler of the feast had tasted the water that was made wine . . . he saith unto him, Every man at the beginning doth set forth good wine . . . but thou hast kept the good wine until now. This beginning of miracles did Jesus in Cana of Galilee" (John 2:7-10).

For *Meister Eckhart*, see editor's note for "*Gnosis*: Language of the Self", p. 62, Note 4.

Note 9: "God is a Spirit: and they that worship Him must worship Him *in spirit and in truth*" (John 4:24).

Louis IX (1214-70) was King of France from 1226.

"*The letter killeth, but the spirit giveth life*" (2 Cor. 3:6).

Note 10: The Eucharistic theology of *Clement of Alexandria* (see editor's note for "*Gnosis*: Language of the Self", p. 61, Note 1) is to be found in his *Stromateis* or "Miscellaneous Studies".

108: Referring to love of God and love of neighbor, Christ said, "On these two commandments hang *all the law and the prophets*" (Matt. 22:40).

For the *Golden Legend*, see editor's note for "The Sense of the Absolute in Religions", p. 12.

Ignatius of Antioch (c. 35-c. 107), the successor of Saint Peter as Bishop of Antioch, was an early Christian martyr.

109: Note 11: *Catherine dei Ricci* (1522-90) was an Italian visionary known for her visions of the Passion and for bearing Christ's stigmata.

For the *Jesus Prayer*, see editor's note for "Vicissitudes of Spiritual Temperaments", p. 46, Note 14; also below in the author's own note.

John *Cassian* (c. 360-435), who was much influenced as a young man by his contact with the Desert Fathers of Egypt (see editor's note for "Vicissitudes of Spiritual Temperaments", p. 35, Note 3), later founded monasteries near Marseilles, transmitting the ascetical and mystical teachings of the East to the Western Church.

In the traditional Latin Mass, the celebrant recites the words *Panem celestem accipiam et nomen Domini invocabo* ("I will receive the Bread of Heaven and call upon the Name of the Lord") and *Calicem salutaris accipiam et nomen Domini invocabo* ("I will receive the Chalice of Salvation and call upon the Name of the Lord") as he prepares to receive the Eucharist.

The *Small Schema* and the *Great Schema* (*schêma* meaning "habit" in Greek) are successive grades of monastic life in the Christian East, each involving solemn vows.

"*The word of God* is quick, and powerful, and sharper than any two-edged sword, piercing even to the dividing asunder of soul and spirit, and of the joints and marrow, and is a discerner of the thoughts and intents of the heart" (Heb. 4:12).

Mary *Consolata of Testona* (1903-46) was an Italian Capuchin nun, whose *prayer of the heart*, received from Christ himself, consisted of the words, "Jesus, Mary, I love you! Save souls!"; her life and teaching are recorded in the book *Jesus Appeals to the World*, published by Lorenzo Sales, I.M.C., in 1955.

110: *Washing of the feet*: "He riseth from supper, and laid aside his garments; and took a towel, and girded himself. After that he poureth water into a basin, and began to wash the disciples' feet, and to wipe them with the towel wherewith he was girded" (John 13:4-5).

Cry of abandonment on the cross: "And about the ninth hour Jesus cried with a loud voice, saying, Eli, Eli, lama sabachthani? that is to say, My God, my God, why hast thou forsaken me?" (Matt. 27:46; cf. Mark 15:34, Ps. 22:1).

Note 12: The author discusses the virtue of humility at length in his *Spiritual Perspectives and Human Facts* (see editor's note for "The Doctrine of Illusion", p. 57, Note 8), Part 6.

Note 13: "The Son of Man came not *to be served but to serve*, and to give his life a ransom for many" (Matt. 20:28).

110-11: Note 13 (cont.): "*Whosoever therefore shall humble himself as this little child, the same is greatest in the kingdom of heaven*" (Matt. 18:4).

111: *Benedict* of Nursia (c. 480-c. 550), known as the "patriarch of Western monasticism", composed a short *Rule* for his monks, which drew upon the spiritual practice of the Desert Fathers and an earlier rule of John Cassian and which gave special emphasis to the virtues of obedience and humility.

For *Bernard* of Clairvaux, see editor's note for "Is There a Natural Mysticism?", p. 28, Note 4.

Note 13 (cont.): "[The scribes and the Pharisees] love *the uppermost rooms at feasts*" (Matt. 23:6, Mark 12:39; cf. Luke 11:43).

Thomas Aquinas (see editor's note for "Vicissitudes of Spiritual Temperaments", p. 49, Note 18) discussed the virtue of humility in his "Treatise on the Virtues" in the *Summa Theologica*.

Note 14: *"Why callest thou me good? There is none good but one, that is, God"* (Matt. 19:17, Mark 10:18; cf. Luke 18:19).

112: According to *Augustine*, "All the divine precepts are referred back to *love*, of which the Apostle [Paul] says, 'Now the end of the commandment is love, out of a pure heart, and a good conscience and a faith unfeigned' (1 Tim. 1:5). Thus every commandment harks back to love" (*Enchiridion*, 32).

"And the light shineth in darkness; and the darkness comprehended it not" (John 1:5).

"Judge not, that ye be not judged" (Matt. 7:1).

"He ascended into Heaven, and sitteth on the right hand of God the Father Almighty: from thence He shall come to *judge the quick and the dead*" (Apostles' Creed).

For *Cabalists*, see editor's note for "The Sense of the Absolute in Religions", p. 10, Note 4.

113: "There is one lawgiver, who is able to save and to destroy: *Who art thou that judgest another?*" (James 4:12; cf. Rom. 14:4).

Wisdom of serpents: "I send you forth as sheep in the midst of wolves: be ye therefore wise as serpents, and harmless as doves" (Matt. 10:16).

"There are diversities of gifts, but the same Spirit. . . . For to one is given by the Spirit the word of wisdom . . . to another *discerning of spirits*" (1 Cor. 12:4, 8, 10).

Note 15: *Impediment of speech from which Moses suffered*: "And Moses said unto the Lord, O my Lord, I am not eloquent, neither heretofore, nor since thou hast spoken unto thy servant: but I am slow of speech, and of a slow tongue. And the Lord said unto him, Who hath made man's mouth? or who maketh the dumb, or deaf, or seeing, or the blind? have not I the Lord? Now therefore go, and I will be with thy mouth, and teach thee what thou shalt say" (Exod. 4:10-12).

115: Note 18: For the *Pauline doctrine of charity*, see the end of the present chapter.

Note 19: René *Descartes* (1596-1650) propounded a method based upon a systematic doubting of everything except one's own self-consciousness, as summed up in the phrase *cogito ergo sum* ("I think; therefore I am").

Immanuel *Kant* (1724-1804), founder of the "critical" philosophy, insisted that man's knowledge is limited to the domain of sensible objects and that the idea of God is no more than a postulate of reason having no objective certainty.

116: "*One thing* is *needful*: and Mary hath chosen that good part, which shall not be taken from her" (Luke 10:42; cf. John 11:1-2).

Christic and Virginal Mysteries

119: *Ave Maria gratia plena, Dominus tecum: benedicta tu in mulieribus, et benedictus fructus ventris tui, Jesus*: these are the words of the Angelical Salutation, or "Hail Mary", in the Latin Rosary: "Hail Mary, full of grace, the Lord is with thee; blessed art thou amongst women, and blessed is the fruit of thy womb, Jesus" (cf. Luke 1:28, 42).

Note 1: *Dominic* (1170-1221), founder of the Order of Friars Preachers, is traditionally held to have instituted the devotion of the Rosary.

The title of the anonymous work *La solide Dévotion du Rosaire* may be rendered as "True Devotion of the Rosary".

122: As themes for meditation in traditional Catholic devotion, the five *joyful mysteries of Mary* are the Annunciation, Visitation, Nativity of Christ, Presentation of Christ in the Temple, and Finding of the

Child Jesus in the Temple; the five *sorrowful mysteries* are the Agony in Gethsemane, Scourging, Crowning with Thorns, Carrying of the Cross, and Crucifixion; and the five *glorious mysteries* are the Resurrection, Ascension, Descent of the Holy Spirit at Pentecost, Assumption of Mary, and Coronation of Mary.

123: For Christ's *state of abandonment*, see editor's note for "Some Observations", p. 110.

The Lord's Prayer: "Our Father which art in heaven, Hallowed be thy Name. Thy kingdom come. Thy will be done in earth, as it is in heaven. Give us this day our daily bread. And forgive us our debts, as we forgive our debtors. And lead us not into temptation, but deliver us from evil: For thine is the kingdom, and the power, and the glory, for ever. Amen" (Matt. 6:9-13).

"*God and His Name are identical*" was the teaching of Ramakrishna (see editor's note for "Vicissitudes of Spiritual Temperaments", p. 39, Note 7).

Pater is the first word in the Latin *Pater Noster*, that is, the "Our Father" or Lord's Prayer, which is recited once for each ten recitations of the *Ave Maria* in the traditional use of the Rosary.

124: Note 3: The Tibetan Buddhist formulation *Om mani padme hum* is a *mantra* meaning "O Thou Jewel in the Lotus, hail".

The Cross

125: "Go thy way, sell whatsoever thou hast, and give to the poor, and thou shalt have treasure in heaven: and come, *take up the cross*, and follow me" (Mark 10:21).

Offer the other cheek: "Unto him that smiteth thee on the one cheek offer also the other" (Luke 6:29).

"We preach Christ crucified, unto the Jews a stumbling-block, and unto the Greeks *foolishness*" (1 Cor. 1:23).

"And the *Word* was *made flesh*, and dwelt among us" (John 1:14).

"If ye live *after the flesh*, ye shall die: but if ye through the Spirit do mortify the deeds of the body, ye shall live" (Rom. 8:13).

Jesus as *the new Adam*: "The first man Adam was made a living soul; the last Adam was made a quickening spirit" (1 Cor. 15:45).

126: "Why callest thou me good? *There is none good but one, that is, God*" (Matt. 19:17, Mark 10:18; cf. Luke 18:19).

"My kingdom is *not of this world*" (John 18:36).

"*Render therefore unto Caesar the things which are Caesar's*" (Matt. 22:21; cf. Mark 12:17, Luke 20:25).

Note 2: *Gregory the Great* (c. 540-604) was Pope from 590.

Bede (c. 673-735), styled "the Venerable", was a monastic scholar, whose *Ecclesiastical History of the English Church and People* was completed in 731.

127: *Offence*: "It is impossible but that offences will come: but woe unto him through whom they come" (Luke 17:1; cf. Matt. 18:7).

"Why beholdest thou the *mote* that is in thy brother's eye, but considerest not the *beam* that is in thine own eye?" (Matt. 7:3; cf. Luke 6:42).

Forgives all: "Beareth all things, believeth all things, hopeth all things, endureth all things" (1 Cor. 13:7).

"*He that is without sin among you, let him first cast a stone*" (John 8:7).

"The wind bloweth where it listeth, and thou hearest the sound thereof, but canst not *tell whence it cometh, and whither it goeth*: so is every one that is born of the Spirit" (John 3:8).

"If any man come to me, and *hate* not his *father, and mother,* and wife, and children, and brethren, and sisters, yea, and his own life also, he cannot be my disciple" (Luke 14:26).

"*One thing* is *needful:* and Mary hath chosen that good part, which shall not be taken away from her" (Luke 10:42; cf. John 11:1-2).

128: *Broad way, narrow way:* "Enter ye in at the strait gate: for wide is the gate, and broad is the way, that leadeth to destruction, and many there be which go in thereat: because strait is the gate, and narrow is the way, which leadeth unto life, and few there be that find it" (Matt. 7:13-14).

Discern spirits: "There are diversities of gifts, but the same Spirit. . . . For to one is given by the Spirit the word of wisdom . . . to another *discerning of spirits*" (1 Cor. 12:4, 8, 10).

"Whosoever shall not receive the kingdom of God *as a little child*, he shall not enter therein" (Mark 10:15; cf. Luke 18:17).

"My kingdom is not *of this world*" (John 18:36).

"*My yoke is easy, and my burden is light*" (Matt. 11:30).

According to tradition, *Longinus* was the soldier who pierced the side of Christ with his spear (cf. John 19:34).

Appendix: Selections from Letters and Other Previously Unpublished Writings

133: Selection 1: Letter of 29 May 1964.

134: Selection 2: Unpublished "Comments", Spring 1963.

The Catholic *Council of Trent* (1545-63), which was convened in response to the Reformation, aimed to eliminate abuses in the Church and to put forward a comprehensive system of Catholic doctrine and practice.

The teaching of *Meister Eckhart* (see editor's note for "*Gnosis*: Language of the Self", p. 62, Note 4) that "there is something in the soul that is uncreated and uncreatable . . . and this is the Intellect" was among the articles for which he was charged with heresy and which he himself subsequently retracted "insofar as they could generate in the minds of the faithful a heretical opinion" (The Bull *In agro dominico* [1329]).

For *al-Hallaj*, see editor's note for "*Gnosis*: Language of the Self", p. 65, Note 9.

Angelus Silesius (see editor's note for "*Gnosis*: Language of the Self", p. 72, Note 17) published a cycle of mystical poems under the title *Cherubinischer Wandersmann*, "The Cherubinic Wanderer", in 1675.

"*It must needs be that offenses come*; but woe to that man by whom the offence cometh" (Matt. 18:7; cf. Luke 17:1).

"*Go ye therefore, and teach all nations*, baptizing them in the name of the Father, and of the Son, and of the Holy Spirit: teaching them to observe all things whatsoever I have commanded you" (Matt. 28:19-20).

135: "*Pearls and swine*": "Give not that which is holy unto the dogs, neither cast ye your pearls before swine, lest they trample them under their feet, and turn again and rend you" (Matt. 7:6).

Selection 3: "The Book of Keys", No. 1054, "God-Consciousness".

Selection 4: Letter of 21 November 1975.

"*One thing* is *needful*: and Mary hath chosen that good part, which shall not be taken from her" (Luke 10:42; cf. John 11:1-2).

136: "*Pray without ceasing*" (1 Thess. 5:17).

Selection 5: Letter of 26 February 1963.

For *Amida*, see editor's note for "Is There a Natural Mysticism?", p. 29.

137: *The Buddhist Sects of Japan: Their History, Philosophical Doctrines, and Sanctuaries* by E. *Steinilber-Oberlin* and Kuni Matsuo was published in 1938.

In speaking of "the *Tarîqah*" the author is referring to the *Tarîqah Maryamiyyah*, a branch of the traditional Shadhiliyyah-Darqawiyyah Sufi lineage for which he served as *Shaykh* for over sixty years.

The *six themes of meditation*, which are outlined in the final chapter of the author's book *Stations of Wisdom* (Bloomington, Indiana: World Wisdom Books, 1995, pp. 147-57), are an important dimension of his spiritual method and include as points of reference: Purity, Act, Peace, Love, Knowledge, and Being.

For *Shinran*, see editor's note for "Vicissitudes of Spiritual Temperaments", p. 46, Note 15.

Selection 6: Letter of 7 October 1960.

139: Selection 7: "The Book of Keys", No. 841, "Space, Time, Existence, Consciousness".

Selection 8: Letter of 21 November 1975.

According to René *Guénon* (see editor's note for "*Gnosis*: Language of the Self", p. 68, Note 13), "The influence that operates through the medium of the Christian sacraments, having originally acted in the initiatic order . . . subsequently . . . lowered its action to the simply religious and exoteric domain" (see "Christianity and Initiation" in Guénon's *Insights into Christian Esoterism* [Hillsdale, New York: Sophia Perennis, 2004]); this claim was strongly repudiated by the author, who insisted on the contrary, "We see absolutely no reason for this 'lowering' in a case like that of Christianity, for the Spirit can in any event proportion its activity according to the capacity of the human receptacle; is God so poor that He would need to ration His graces after having granted them? Why should not one and the same rite be able to confer individual help to one and supra-individual help to another? For he who can do the greater can do the lesser" (*René Guénon: Some Observations* [Hillsdale, New York: Sophia Perennis, 2004], p. 41).

141: Selection 9: Letter, c. 1960.

"Behold, *the kingdom of God is within you*" (Luke 17:21).

For Mary *Consolata*, see editor's note for "Some Observations", p. 109, Note 11.

142: Selection 10: Letter of 21 May 1961.

The *Shaykh* Ahmad *al-Alawi* (1869-1934), a famous Algerian Sufi *shaykh*, was Schuon's spiritual master.

For Guénon and hence the *Guénonian "believer"*, the term "religion" is reserved for the exoterism of the Abrahamic traditions, in which salvation is understood to consist in the preservation or perpetuation of the human individual rather than in his final deliverance from individuality as such, and in which the word "God" is ordinarily limited to its ontological or personal meaning.

143: Selection 11: "The Book of Keys", No. 981, "Criteria of the Spiritual Man".

144: Selection 12: Letter of 19 July 1974.

Selection 13: Letter of 2 June 1974.

144-45: According to *Plato* (see editor's note for "*Gnosis*: Language of the Self", p. 68), a world of eternal Forms or Ideas exists "above" the world of change and multiplicity, these Forms serving as *models* or archetypes of their temporal copies, and yet the Forms are themselves "below" the supreme Reality, which Plato called the Good.

145: *Gregory Palamas* (c. 1296-1359), a monk of Mount Athos, is best known for his defense of the psychosomatic contemplative techniques employed by the Hesychast Fathers (see editor's note for "Is There a Natural Mysticism?", p. 29, Note 5).

According to *Pythagoras* of Samos (c. 569-c. 475 B.C.), one of the greatest sages of ancient Greece, everything in the universe is made of Numbers, all things being modeled or patterned by proportion and ratio.

Socrates (c. 470-399 B.C.), proclaimed by the Delphic Oracle to be the wisest man in the world, was the teacher of Plato.

Selection 14: "The Book of Keys", No. 735, "To Avoid the Snare of Signs".

146: Selection 15: Letter of November 1932.

147: *The words of the crucified Christ to Saint John*: "When Jesus therefore saw his mother, and the disciple standing by, whom he loved, he saith unto his mother, Woman, behold thy son! Then saith he to the disciple, Behold thy mother! And from that hour that disciple took her unto his own home" (John 19:26-27).

148: *In ipso vita erat, et vita erat lux hominum. Et lux in tenebris lucet, et tenebrae eam non comprehenderunt* is the text of John 1:4-5 in the Latin Vulgate: "In him was life; and the life was the light of men. And the light shineth in darkness; and the darkness comprehended it not."

Selection 16: "The Book of Keys", No. 3, "The Wheel".

For *Shankara*, see editor's note for "Is There a Natural Mysticism?", p. 27.

"*I sleep, but my heart waketh*" (Song of Sol. 5:2).

GLOSSARY OF FOREIGN TERMS AND PHRASES

Advaita (Sanskrit): "non-dualist" interpretation of the *Vedânta*; Hindu doctrine according to which the seeming multiplicity of things is regarded as the product of ignorance, the only true reality being *Brahma*, the One, the Absolute, the Infinite, which is the unchanging ground of appearance.

Alter (Latin): the "other", in contrast to the *ego* or individual self.

Amor (Latin): "love".

Ânanda (Sanskrit): "bliss, beatitude, joy"; one of the three essential aspects of *Apara-Brahma*, together with *Sat*, "being", and *Chit*, "consciousness".

Anima (Latin): the "soul" (feminine) as the breath of life or vital principle of the physical body.

Animus (Latin): the "soul" (masculine) as the seat of the mind or rational principle.

Apara-Brahma (Sanskrit): the "non-supreme" or penultimate *Brahma*, also called *Brahma saguna*; in Schuon's teaching, the "relative Absolute"; see *para-Brahma*.

Ascesis (Greek): "exercise, practice, training", as of an athlete; a regimen of self-denial, especially one involving fasting, prostrations, and other bodily disciplines.

Âtmâ or *Âtman* (Sanskrit): the real or true "Self", underlying the ego and its manifestations; in the perspective of *Advaita Vedânta*, identical with *Brahma*.

Avatâra (Sanskrit): the earthly "descent", incarnation, or manifestation of God, especially of Vishnu in the Hindu tradition.

Ave Maria (Latin): "Hail, Mary"; traditional prayer to the Blessed Virgin, also known as the Angelic Salutation, based on the words of the Archangel Gabriel and Saint Elizabeth in Luke 1:28, 42.

181

Barakah (Arabic): "blessing", grace; in Islam, a spiritual influence or energy emanating originally from God, but often attached to sacred objects and spiritual persons.

Bhakta (Sanskrit): a follower of the spiritual path of *bhakti*; a person whose relationship with God is based primarily on adoration and love.

Bhakti, bhakti-mârga (Sanskrit): the spiritual "path" (*mârga*) of "love" (*bhakti*) and devotion; see *jnâna* and *karma*.

Bodhisattva (Sanskrit, Pali): literally, "enlightenment-being"; in *Mahâyâna* Buddhism, one who postpones his own final enlightenment and entry into *Nirvâna* in order to aid all other sentient beings in their quest for Buddhahood.

Brahma or *Brahman* (Sanskrit): the Supreme Reality, the Absolute.

Brahmâ (Sanskrit): God in the aspect of Creator, the first divine "person" of the *Trimûrti*; to be distinguished from *Brahma*, the Supreme Reality.

Buddhi (Sanskrit): "Intellect"; the highest faculty of knowledge, to be contrasted with *manas*, that is, mind or reason.

Chit (Sanskrit): "consciousness"; one of the three essential aspects of *Apara-Brahma*, together with *Sat*, "being", and *Ânanda*, "bliss, beatitude, joy".

Christe eleison (Greek): "Christ, have mercy"; used antiphonally with the words *Kyrie eleison*, "Lord, have mercy", in the Roman rite.

Creatio ex nihilo (Latin): "creation out of nothing"; the doctrine that God Himself is the sufficient cause of the universe, needing nothing else; often set in contrast to emanationist cosmogonies.

Dhamma (Pali): same as *dharma* in Buddhism.

Dharma (Sanskrit): in Hinduism, the underlying "law" or "order" of the cosmos as expressed in sacred rites and in actions appropriate to various social relationships and human vocations; in Buddhism, the practice and realization of Truth.

Dhikr (Arabic): "remembrance" of God, based upon the repeated invocation of His Name; central to Sufi practice, where the remembrance is often supported by the single word *Allâh*.

Dîn (Arabic): "religion"; the exoteric tradition of Islam.

Ego-alter (Latin): "I-other".

Ex divinis (Latin): literally, "from divine things"; coming forth from the Divine, or from the divine Principle; the plural form is used insofar as the Principle comprises both *Para-Brahma*, Beyond-Being or the Absolute, and *Apara-Brahma*, Being or the relative Absolute.

Fanâ' (Arabic): "extinction, annihilation, evanescence"; in Sufism, the spiritual station or degree of realization in which all individual attributes and limitations are extinguished in union with God; see *Nirvâna*.

Faqr (Arabic): "indigence, spiritual poverty"; the virtue cultivated by the Sufi *faqîr*, the "poor one", whose self-effacement testifies to complete dependence on God and a desire to be filled by Him alone.

Fâtihah (Arabic): the "opening" *sûrah*, or chapter, of the Koran, recited in the daily prayers of all Muslims and consisting of the words: "In the Name of God, the Beneficent, the Merciful. Praise to God, Lord of the Worlds, the Beneficent, the Merciful. Owner of the Day of Judgment, Thee (alone) we worship; Thee (alone) we ask for help. Show us the straight path, the path of those whom Thou hast favored, not (the path) of those who earn Thine anger, nor of those who go astray."

Fiat lux (Latin): "Let there be light" (cf. Gen. 1:3).

Filioque (Latin): "and (from) the Son"; a term added to the Nicene Creed by the Western Church to express the "double procession" of the Holy Spirit from the Father "and the Son"; rejected by the Eastern Orthodox Church.

Gnosis (Greek): "knowledge"; spiritual insight, principial comprehension, divine wisdom.

Gopi (Sanskrit): literally, "keeper of the cows"; in Hindu tradition, one of the cowherd girls involved with Krishna in the love affairs of his youth, symbolic of the soul's devotion to God.

Guna (Sanskrit): literally, "strand"; quality, characteristic, attribute; in Hinduism, the *guna*s are the three constituents of *Prakriti*: *sattva* (the ascending, luminous quality), *rajas* (the expansive, passional quality), and *tamas* (the descending, dark quality).

Hadîth (Arabic, plural *ahâdîth*): "saying, narrative"; an account of the words or deeds of the Prophet Muhammad, transmitted through a traditional chain of known intermediaries.

Hari (Sanskrit): in Hinduism, the means by which *Brahma* becomes manifest; an epithet for God in any of His personal forms.

Hic jacet nemo (Latin): "Here lies no one", used as an epitaph.

In divinis (Latin): literally, "in or among divine things"; within the divine Principle; the plural form is used insofar as the Principle comprises both *Para-Brahma*, Beyond-Being or the Absolute, and *Apara-Brahma*, Being or the relative Absolute.

In shâ'a 'Llâh (Arabic): "If God should so will".

Îshvara (Sanskrit): one who "possesses power"; God understood as a personal being, as Creator and Lord; manifest in the *Trimûrti* as *Brahmâ*, *Vishnu*, and *Shiva*.

al-Islâm (Arabic): "surrender, submission, peace"; the condition of peace resulting from faithful submission to God.

Japa-Yoga (Sanskrit): method of "union" or "unification" (*yoga*) based upon the "repetition" (*japa*) of a *mantra* or sacred formula, often containing one of the Names of God.

Jejunium (Latin): "fasting, abstinence from food".

Jnâna or *jnâna-mârga* (Sanskrit): the spiritual "path" (*mârga*) of "knowledge" (*jnâna*) and intellection; see *bhakti* and *karma*.

Jnânin (Sanskrit): a follower of the path of *jnâna*; a person whose relationship with God is based primarily on sapiential knowledge or *gnosis*.

Jôdo-Shinshû (Japanese): "true pure land school"; a sect of Japanese Pure Land Buddhism founded by Shinran, based on faith in the power of the Buddha Amida and characterized by use of the *nembutsu*.

Kali-Yuga (Sanskrit): in Hinduism, the fourth and final *yuga* in a given cycle of time, corresponding to the Iron Age of Western tradition; the present age of mankind, distinguished by its increasing disorder, violence, and forgetfulness of God.

Kalki-Avatâra (Sanskrit): the tenth and last of the incarnations of Vishnu, who is to come at the end of the *Kali-Yuga* in order to punish evildoers and usher in a new age.

Karma (Sanskrit): "action, work"; in Hinduism and Buddhism, the law of consequence, in which the present is explained by reference to the nature and quality of one's past actions; one of the principal *mârga*s or spiritual "paths" of Hinduism, characterized by its stress on righteous deeds; see *bhakti* and *jnâna*.

Kôan (Japanese): literally, "precedent for public use", case study; in Zen Buddhism, a question or anecdote often based on the experience or sayings of a notable master and involving a paradox or puzzle that cannot be solved in conventional terms or with ordinary thinking.

Krita-Yuga (Sanskrit): in Hinduism, the first *yuga* in a given cycle of time; the Golden Age or Eden of Western tradition, distinguished by *rita*, that is, "order, justice".

Lâ ilâha illâ 'Llâh (Arabic): "There is no god but God"; see *Shahâdah*.

Logos (Greek): "word, reason"; in Christian theology, the divine, uncreated Word of God (cf. John 1:1); the transcendent Principle of creation and revelation.

Mahabbah (Arabic): "love"; in Sufism, the spiritual way based upon love and devotion, analogous to the Hindu *bhakti mârga*; see *makhâfah* and *ma'rifah*.

Makhâfah (Arabic): "fear"; in Sufism, the spiritual way based upon the fear of God, analogous to the Hindu *karma mârga*; see *mahabbah* and *ma'rifah*.

Mahâpralaya (Sanskrit): in Hinduism, the "great" or final "dissolving" of the universe at the end of a *kalpa*, or "day in the life of *Brahmâ*", understood as lasting one thousand *yuga*s; see *pralaya*.

Mahâyâna (Sanskrit): "great vehicle"; the form of Buddhism, including such traditions as Zen and *Jôdo-Shinshû*, which regards itself as the fullest or most adequate expression of the Buddha's teaching; distinguished by the idea that *Nirvâna* is not other than *samsâra* truly seen as it is.

Mantra (Sanskrit): "instrument of thought"; a word or phrase of divine origin, often including a Name of God, repeated by those initiated into its proper use as a means of salvation or liberation; see *japa-yoga*.

Ma'rifah (Arabic): "knowledge"; in Sufism, the spiritual way based upon knowledge or *gnosis*, analogous to the Hindu *jnâna-mârga*; see *mahabbah* and *makhâfah*.

Materia prima (Latin): "first or prime matter"; in Platonic cosmology, the undifferentiated and primordial substance serving as a "receptacle" for the shaping force of divine Forms or Ideas; universal potentiality.

Mâyâ (Sanskrit): "artifice, illusion"; in *Advaita Vedânta*, the beguiling concealment of *Brahma* in the form or under the appearance of a lower reality.

Mors (Latin): "death".

Mûla-Prakriti (Sanskrit): literally, "root-nature"; in Hindu cosmology, undifferentiated primordial substance.

Nâma-rûpa (Sanskrit): literally, "name-form"; in Hinduism, the seemingly substantial appearance with which *Mâyâ* clothes itself.

Nembutsu (Japanese): "remembrance or mindfulness of the Buddha", based upon the repeated invocation of his Name; same as *buddhânusmriti* in Sanskrit and *nien-fo* in Chinese.

Nirvâna (Sanskrit): "blowing out, extinction"; in Indian traditions, especially Buddhism, the extinction of the fires of passion and the resulting, supremely blissful state of liberation from egoism and attachment; see *fanâ*.

Oratio (Latin): literally, "language, speech"; in Christian usage, words addressed to God; prayer.

Para-Brahma (Sanskrit): the "supreme" or ultimate *Brahma*, also called *Brahma nirguna*; the Absolute as such; see *apara-Brahma*.

Paramâtmâ or *Paramâtman* (Sanskrit): the "supreme Self".

Philosophia perennis (Latin): "perennial philosophy".

Pontifex Maximus (Latin): "supreme pontiff"; a phrase claiming for the Bishop of Rome (the Pope) the right of universal jurisdiction over the entire Church, both East and West.

Prakriti (Sanskrit): literally, "making first" (see *materia prima*); the fundamental, "feminine" substance or material cause of all things; see *Purusha*.

Pralaya (Sanskrit): "dissolution"; Hindu teaching that all appearance is subject to a periodic process of destruction and recreation; see *mahâpralaya*.

Primus inter pares (Latin): "first among equals"; a phrase acknowledging the primacy of honor traditionally accorded to the Bishop of Rome (the Pope) in relation to the patriarchs of the other ancient sees of the Church.

Purusha (Sanskrit): "man"; the informing or shaping principle of creation; the "masculine" demiurge or fashioner of the universe; see *Prakriti*.

Rajas (Sanskrit): in Hinduism, one of the three *guna*s, or qualities, of *Prakriti*, of which all things are woven; the quality of expansiveness, manifest in the material world as force or movement and in the soul as ambition, initiative, and restlessness.

Religio (Latin): "religion", often in reference to its exoteric dimension.

Sannyâsa or *samnyâsa* (Sanskrit): "renunciation"; in Hindu tradition, the formal breaking of all ties to family, caste, and property at the outset of the final stage of life.

Sannyâsin (Sanskrit): "renunciate"; in Hindu tradition, one who has renounced all formal ties to social life.

Sat (Sanskrit): "being"; one of the three essential aspects of *Apara-Brahma*, together with *Chit*, "consciousness", and *Ânanda*, "bliss, beatitude, joy".

Sat-Chit-Ânanda or *Sachchidânanda* (Sanskrit): "being-consciousness-bliss"; the three essential aspects of *Apara-Brahma*, that is, *Brahma* insofar as it can be grasped in human experience.

Sattva (Sanskrit): in Hinduism, one of the three *guna*s, or qualities, of *Prakriti*, of which all things are woven; the quality of luminosity, manifest in the material world as buoyancy or lightness and in the soul as intelligence and virtue.

Sephiroth or *sefirot* (Hebrew): literally, "numbers"; in Jewish Cabala, the ten emanations of *Ein Sof* or divine Infinitude, each comprising a different aspect of creative energy.

Shahâdah (Arabic): the fundamental "profession" or "testimony" of faith in Islam, consisting of the words *Lâ ilâha illâ 'Llâh, Muhammadan rasûlu 'Llâh*: "There is no god but God; Muhammad is the messenger of God."

Shâstra (Sanskrit): "command, rule"; traditional Hindu book of law.

Shinshû (Japanese): see *Jôdo-Shinshû*.

Sophia (Greek): "wisdom"; in Jewish and Christian tradition, the Wisdom of God, often conceived as feminine (cf. Prov. 8).

Spiritus (Latin): "spirit"; the supra-individual principle of the human microcosm, with its seat in the heart.

Spiritus Sanctus (Latin): the "Holy Spirit"; in Christian theology, the third Person of the Trinity.

Sub omni caelo (Latin): literally, "under all the heaven", that is, everywhere.

Sunnah (Arabic): "custom, way of acting"; in Islam, the norm established by the Prophet Muhammad, including his actions and sayings (see *hadîth*) and serving as a precedent and standard for the behavior of Muslims.

Sûtra (Sanskrit): literally, "thread"; a Hindu or Buddhist sacred text; in Hinduism, any short, aphoristic verse or collection of verses, often elliptical in style; in Buddhism, a collection of the discourses of the Buddha.

Tamas (Sanskrit): in Hinduism, one of the three *guna*s, or qualities, of *Prakriti*, of which all things are woven; the quality of darkness or heaviness, manifest in the material world as inertia or rigidity and in the soul as sloth, stupidity, and vice.

Tarîqah (Arabic): "path"; in exoteric Islam, a virtual synonym for *sharî'ah*, equivalent to the "straight path" mentioned in the *Fâtihah*; in Sufism, the mystical path leading from observance of the *sharî'ah* to self-realization in God; also a Sufi brotherhood.

Tasawwuf (Arabic): a term of disputed etymology, though perhaps from *sûf* for "wool", after the garment worn by many early Sufis; traditional Muslim word for Sufism.

Tathâgata (Sanskrit): literally, "thus gone" or "thus come"; according to Buddhist tradition, the title the Buddha chose for himself, interpreted to mean: he who has won through to the supreme liberation; he who has come with the supreme teaching; he who has gone before and found the true path.

Torah (Hebrew): "instruction, teaching"; in Judaism, the written law of God, as revealed to Moses on Sinai and embodied in the Pentateuch (Genesis, Exodus, Leviticus, Numbers, Deuteronomy).

Trimûrti (Sanskrit): literally, "having three forms"; in Hindu tradition, a triadic expression of the Divine, especially in the form of *Brahmâ*, the creator, *Vishnu*, the preserver, and *Shiva*, the transformer.

'Ulamâ' (Arabic, singular *'alîm*): "those who know, scholars"; in Islam, those who are learned in matters of law and theology; traditional authorities for all aspects of Muslim life.

Vacare Deo (Latin): literally, "to be empty for God"; to be at leisure for or available to God; in the Christian monastic and contemplative tradition, to set aside time from work for meditation and prayer.

Vedânta (Sanskrit): "end or culmination of the Vedas"; one of the major schools of traditional Hindu philosophy, based in part on the Upanishads, esoteric treatises found at the conclusion of the Vedic scriptures; see *advaita*.

Yoga (Sanskrit): literally, "yoking, union"; in Indian traditions, any meditative and ascetic technique designed to bring the soul and body into a state of concentration.

Yogin (Sanskrit): one who is "yoked or joined"; a practitioner of *yoga*.

Yuga (Sanskrit): an "age" in Hinduism; one of the four periods into which a cycle of time is divided.

INDEX

For a glossary of all key foreign words used in books published by World Wisdom, including metaphysical terms in English, consult: www.DictionaryofSpiritualTerms.org.
This on-line Dictionary of Spiritual Terms provides extensive definitions, examples and related terms in other languages.

BIOGRAPHICAL NOTES

Frithjof Schuon

Born in Basle, Switzerland in 1907, Frithjof Schuon was the twentieth century's preeminent spokesman for the perennialist school of comparative religious thought.

The leitmotif of Schuon's work was foreshadowed in an encounter during his youth with a marabout who had accompanied some members of his Senegalese village to Basle for the purpose of demonstrating their African culture. When Schuon talked with him, the venerable old man drew a circle with radii on the ground and explained: "God is the center; all paths lead to Him." Until his later years Schuon traveled widely, from India and the Middle East to America, experiencing traditional cultures and establishing lifelong friendships with Hindu, Buddhist, Christian, Muslim, and American Indian spiritual leaders.

A philosopher in the tradition of Plato, Shankara, and Eckhart, Schuon was a gifted artist and poet as well as the author of over twenty books on religion, metaphysics, sacred art, and the spiritual path. Describing his first book, *The Transcendent Unity of Religions*, T. S. Eliot wrote, "I have met with no more impressive work in the comparative study of Oriental and Occidental religion", and world-renowned religion scholar Huston Smith said of Schuon, "The man is a living wonder; intellectually apropos religion, equally in depth and breadth, the paragon of our time". Schuon's books have been translated into over a dozen languages and are respected by academic and religious authorities alike.

More than a scholar and writer, Schuon was a spiritual guide for seekers from a wide variety of religions and backgrounds throughout the world. He died in 1998.

James S. Cutsinger (Ph.D., Harvard) is Professor of Theology and Religious Thought at the University of South Carolina.

A widely recognized writer on the *sophia perennis* and the perennialist school, Professor Cutsinger is also an authority on the theology and spirituality of the Christian East. His publications include *Advice to the Serious Seeker: Meditations on the Teaching of Frithjof Schuon, Not of This World: A Treasury of Christian Mysticism, Paths to the Heart: Sufism and the Christian East, The Fullness of God: Frithjof Schuon on Christianity, Prayer Fashions Man: Frithjof Schuon on the Spiritual Life*, and *Splendor of the True: A Frithjof Schuon Reader*.